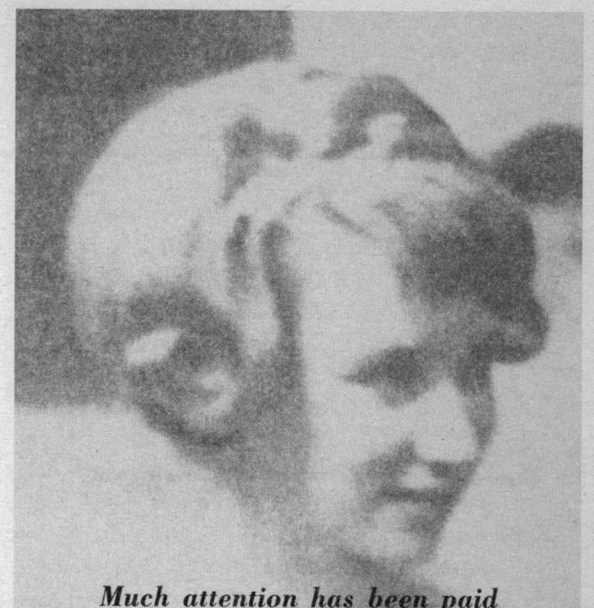

Much attention has been paid to Campbell's shoulders thanks to a single photograph but what about what's above them? Who is Kim Campbell? Does she have what it takes to be a good prime minister?

KIM CAMPBELL

ABOVE THE SHOULDERS

DENNIS BUECKERT

Voyageur Publishing
82 Frontenac Street, Hull, Quebec J8X 1Z5
(819) 778-2946

Editor: Sean Fordyce
Publicist: Elizabeth Jefferson
82 Frontenac Street, Hull, Quebec
J8X 1Z5
(819) 778-2946

Cover and book design: Beth Haliburton/Loco Design

First Edition September, 1993

ISBN 0-921842-32-5

Printed in Canada.

ACKNOWLEDGEMENTS

Research was done in Vancouver by Brent Jang and Daniel Doerksen.

Thanks to Kirk LaPointe, Ottawa Bureau Chief, *The Canadian Press*, for letting me take my holidays on short notice to write this book and to the whole gang at *CP* Ottawa for unfailing humor through thick and thin.

Thanks for criticism, encouragement and suggestions to Rob Russo, Portia Priegert, Warren Caragata, Ross Howard, Claire Hoy, Eoin Kenny, Kathleen O'Hara, Gord McIntosh, Jim Bronskill, Don Friesen, Larry Bencze, Sean Silcoff, Elizabeth Jefferson and Sean Fordyce.

I received invaluable assistance from the Pacific Press library, the Library of Parliament, the Ottawa Public Library and the National Library of Canada.

Everyone knows that writers depend heavily on their publishers but I never expected the amount of support that I had from Sean Fordyce of Voyageur Publishing. Those debates about wording at 3:00 a.m. will no doubt be remembered fondly at some future date, as grueling as they seemed at the time. Sean never lost his patience or his creative energy even when I was exhausted, and if the manuscript passes the test of public scrutiny, he deserves a large share of the credit.

DEDICATION

To that hardy band of workers, entrepreneurs and honest politicians who still struggle for peace, order and sustainable development.

CONTENTS

PREFACE

She came out of the blue — or was it the Big Blue Machine?

Only a few years ago most Canadians would have had trouble identifying Kim Campbell, now she's running the country.

Here's a mystery story to while away a rainy afternoon. How could a virtual unknown rise in the space of five years to the highest position in the land without stating a single clear policy position and with scarcely anyone really knowing who she is?

Some would believe Campbellmania erupted spontaneously from the national psyche like hot lava from a raging volcano. They say it was "spontaneous combustion." Others suspect a sinister plot by the Mulroney brain trust, greased by a gullible media.

Somewhere below the torrents of speculation there must be a bedrock of fact which I hope to expose.

The market for Kim books may seem a bit crowded, since four have appeared recently, but in my cheerfully biased opinion this one will make the others obsolete since it is the most up-to-date and the most concise. Who needs all the boring details? Readers will find the *interesting* details here as well as the major points set out in clear relief; they will find previously unpublished material casting light on key aspects of Campbell's career and they will find the most relevant information that has been uncovered by the collective toil of Canadian journalists since Campbell became a public figure.

I must pay tribute to Robert Fife for his extremely well-researched and thorough biography *Kim Campbell the Making of a Politician*. There's no doubt he had excellent sources in the Tory establishment for he obtained many details which could only have been known by insiders. For example, he is the first to report that Campbell underwent psychiatric treatment during her university days and to confirm that Brian Mulroney favored Campbell in the run-up to the Tory leadership race while publicly claiming to be neutral.

Our books are really complementary, but those who don't want to buy an expensive hard cover can rest assured I've read Fife's book from top to bottom and they won't miss anything by opting for this modest paperback.

One press gallery colleague who saw an early draft of this manuscript complained that it read like wire service copy, "so balanced that it's boring," but I insist there's a great market for unvarnished truth. Journalism doesn't have to be vicious to be good, nor is a convoluted style proof of higher intelligence. Years ago, the wonderful storyteller Morley Callaghan told me the most important thing for a writer is to see with his own eyes, and that's what I've tried to do.

I have studied every shred of evidence that I could find to illuminate the Kim mystery, from her high school poetry to her speeches in the House of Commons. I have admired her finer flights of professorial exposition and shaken my head at her habit of embellishing the facts even when there's nothing to be gained. I have interviewed some of her bitterest enemies and some of her most devoted friends. I have prevailed upon much maligned civil servants to virtually turn the country upside down looking for cardboard boxes of obscure documents. I have drawn extensively from the work of other journalists and have tried to be scrupulous in giving them credit.

Does it really matter whether Campbell speaks Russian? Does it really matter whether she spent her London years at study or at the theatre? Does it really matter whether she took off her blouse for that picture?

Many Canadians feel that when it comes to the prime ministership everything matters, especially the truth. The country is wonderful, precious and fragile. The keys to 24 Sussex should be guarded carefully even if the new occupant brings her own furniture.

CHAPTER 1

ROOTS

Ralph White still has the bracelet Kim Campbell gave him when they were going steady at Prince of Wales Secondary School. He keeps her pictures in a scrapbook. He wonders what happened to the songs they wrote together. And he's convinced she'll make a good Prime Minister.

"It's not just my feeling, but a lot of people who went to school with her think she's the only hope we've got," says White, who dated Campbell through grades nine, ten and part of eleven.

But he worries about her too. Will she be able to cope with the pressures? Will she be able to achieve real change? Will she be reduced to serving as a mouthpiece for the political organization that brought her to power? Will she have time for old friends?

"I guess her timetable now is just packed," says White, who was interviewed during the runup to the leadership convention. "Somebody told me she's only going to be in B.C. for 5.3 days between now and the convention. Everything's all mapped out, I mean it's a big machine. It's almost like we've all lost control. It's kind of a scary thing actually."

Vancouver lawyer Phil Rankin also knows Campbell well but his memories of her aren't so fond. Whenever reporters want an anti-Campbell quote they go to Rankin, who served with her on the Vancouver School Board during the early 1980s. They were members of opposing parties, and he makes no attempt to conceal his bias. He says she is the most egotistical person he ever met.

"She's just been a political hack all her life and we're supposed to be impressed because of her brilliance and her huge capacity of learning and background," says Rankin.

"Her only real craft has been politics. She's never really worked.

"She understands the political system, but the more I understand the political system the more I worry and grieve for humanity."

Campbell seems to spark extreme emotions in people. Her supporters say she's not a typical politician, which is true. There's enough pain and dislocation in her life story to fuel a long novel; there's prodigious success, dismal failure, anguish and loneliness, a courageous refusal to be crushed and, yes, those mysteries.

The story begins in Port Alberni, a small town on the rugged west coast of Vancouver Island, where Campbell was born on March 10, 1947, weighing in at seven pounds, seven ounces. According to a story by Stephen Brunt of the *Globe and Mail*, the birth was induced so it would happen when her father, George Campbell, was home. It's a telling detail, given the increased risk of complications associated with induced births.

Kim's legal name is Avril Phaedra Douglas Campbell. The names were chosen by her mother who had a taste for literature. The second name, Phaedra, is a strange choice. Phaedra is one of the most tragic figures in Greek mythology. She falls in love with her stepson Hippolytus but he rejects her. Furious, she leads King Theseus to believe that Hippolytus has committed an outrage against her. Her deception succeeds and Theseus executes his own son. Phaedra is stricken by guilt, confesses all her sordid machinations and poisons herself. In Racine's celebrated version she literally creeps from the stage, dying. It's not surprising that Campbell does not mention her second name in any public documents.

Campbell's mother, Phyllis Cook, is a sixth-generation Canadian, descended from United Empire Loyalist stock. Her maternal grandfather was born in Nanaimo and her great-great-grandfather came from Nova Scotia to pioneer on

Vancouver Island. Phyllis changed her last name when she remarried, changed her first name by choice, and now is Lissa Vroom. This makes for some confusion, since at various times she was Phyllis Cook, Phyllis Campbell and Lissa Vroom.

Phyllis grew up in Port Alberni where her father was a dentist. After graduating from high school she enlisted in the navy as a Wren (Women's Royal Canadian Naval Service) and served as a wireless operator in Halifax.

Phyllis met George Campbell in 1943 while she was home on leave. He was stationed in Port Alberni as a sergeant-instructor in the Canadian Army, and pursued Phyllis with great determination sending her many letters and gifts. She initially rejected him but finally succumbed only to bitterly regret it later.

"I was bombarded by letters from him constantly, wherever I went," she says. "After a while it began to seem like the only permanent thing in my life was this constant barrage of letters. He began to seem like something to hang on to. I think that's what did it."

They were married in 1944 and Phyllis realized she was pregnant a few months after the wedding. George was overseas when Kim's older sister, Alix Paula Bernadette Campbell, was born. In George's absence, Phyllis and baby Alix lived with Phyllis's mother.

George was posted to England where he joined the Seaforth Highlanders, then to Italy where he was wounded by shrapnel. He spent several years in and out of hospital in Italy and England, then returned to Vancouver Island where he enrolled at Victoria College. He couldn't get accommodation for his family at the college so Phyllis and Alix continued living with Phyllis's mother in Port Alberni.

When George Campbell had sufficiently recovered to work, he got a job as a forestry lookout near Port Alberni. This involved many hours of total solitude at the top of a dizzyingly high structure — madness was an occupational hazard.

Kim Campbell has bragged more than once that she was conceived at the top of a timber lookout, a story which probably should be taken with a grain of salt. It's not implausible that Campbell's parents made love at the top of a lookout, but they probably also did so in their cabin on the ground.

During this time in an isolated mountain cabin, Phyllis came to know what her husband was really like. It apparently was not a pleasant discovery. "It's a shock, when you're young, to realize that you can make really awful mistakes."

Phyllis says she would have preferred not to have another child by George, but her efforts at birth control were unsuccessful. "Unfortunately, in those days, babies came when they wanted to despite all of your clever intentions."

George Campbell wanted to be a doctor but his marks weren't good enough, so he enrolled in law school at the University of British Columbia. The family moved to Vancouver; Phyllis taught herself to type and supported them by working in clerical jobs. "The four of us lived on $92 a month," she recalls.

Child psychologists say the early years of life are crucial to character formation, but little is known about Campbell's infancy and early childhood. Her parents must have faced great challenges raising two infants while George was carrying a full course load at university and Phyllis was working split shifts downtown. How would the family cope with emergencies such as illness in such circumstances?

Kim did in fact have some health problems. When she was not yet two years old her parents were awakened one night by her gasping. When they rushed into her room her face was turning blue. They called the doctor, who summoned an ambulance. At the hospital the doctors performed a tracheotomy and she was kept in isolation for two weeks, apparently in the belief that she had polio, but her condition turned out to be something called septic laryngitis. When her parents collected her after two weeks she treated them like betrayers.

George began law school when Kim was three and Alix was five. The family did not have the money to hire a nanny. Neither George nor Phyllis had close family nearby to help. Worst of all, as Phyllis has made abundantly clear, she and

George didn't get along. But they did stay together until Kim was 12 and Alix 14, and despite everything, Kim has happy memories of her childhood.

"I was raised in Vancouver," she told Peter Newman, in one of the quotes which he chose not to include in his famous *Vancouver Magazine* story about Campbell.

"The first place we lived was in Queen Elizabeth Park which was an old army camp. We lived in huts in Little Mountain Camp I'd guess from 1947 to 1950. In 1950 my parents bought a house out in Burnaby, a little bungalow, which was wonderful because it was very countrified then. We used to climb Burnaby Mountain to pick berries and there was a house next door with a large field. My sister and I were great tomboys. We were quite poor because my dad was a student. We wore jeans and shirts all the time and climbed trees and were quite wild. It was just wonderful."

Once George Campbell had won his law degree he wasted little time getting upwardly mobile. Soon he was a respected prosecutor. The home where Kim Campbell grew up stands at the corner of West 33rd. Avenue and Trafalgar Street. It's a big place in the English Tudor style; half-timbered, with leaded glass windows. The lawn is well tended, enclosed by a hedge and a low stone wall; no sign of trouble anywhere.

The whole neighborhood, named Kerrisdale, looks like it came straight out of a Dick and Jane reader — tall trees, shady lawns, neatly trimmed hedges. A few streets over is Shaughnessy where the really rich people live.

With George making good money, Phyllis set about doing the things she had always wanted to do. She enrolled in the Vancouver School of Art to study portraiture. Alix and Kim took music lessons. Phyllis says Kim could pick out classical tunes at the age of four. It sounds idyllic, but there were powerful tensions in the family.

Phyllis's sister, Shirley McPhail, tells some of the more lurid anecdotes. When George was asked to help with housework he would reply: "That's squaw work!" His presence in the room was enough to trigger an asthmatic attack in little Kim, according to McPhail.

George Campbell's recollections of Kim as a child are remarkably vague. "I don't remember Kim crying very much, whatever that means," he says. Or: "I represent family to her. She (sister Alix) represents best friend." He does recall Kim organizing a roaring '20s chorus line when she was in grade six. "I can remember standing and looking down at this line of dancers kicking their legs and coming on to the patio."

CHAPTER 2

ABANDONNED

Everyone who writes about Kim Campbell faces the difficult problem of how to deal with the divorce of her parents when she was 12. To dwell on it seems indecent, to gloss it over seems irresponsible. Psychologists say that divorce is one of the hardest things that can happen to a child, more stressful even than the death of a parent. There's no question the break-up had a major impact on Campbell.

As Heather Bird of the *Ottawa Sun* puts it, "When the subject arises it is clear the breakup touches places of great pain in the family. George Campbell is obviously uncomfortable but he raises it and is quick to point out it's all in the past. And that they all got through it the best they could."

The first stories about Campbell's childhood suggested that Phyllis left George for no good reason other than boredom with domestic life and a thirst for adventure. Charlotte Gray said in *Saturday Night* that Phyllis "escaped from the dreary domestic trap and disappeared for six years to crew boats in the Mediterranean and West Indies."

Mark Kennedy said in the *Ottawa Citizen* that "Phyllis Campbell was not happy with her life and she decided to leave. (She ended up working as a caretaker on yachts in the Mediterranean and Caribbean.)"

A much different version emerged when Judy Steed of the *Toronto Star* managed to get an interview with Kim's mother. Phyllis, now known as Lissa, told Steed she was tired of seeing "George's smug face on TV" and with being portrayed as a "flighty woman" who'd abandoned her family. The truth was, she said, that she'd been driven into exile by a bad marriage.

"I spent eight years working to put George through university," she told Steed. "I worked in a doctor's office and as a bank manager — the most I earned was $45 a week — and he ended up a lawyer and I ended up with no skills to earn a decent living that would have enabled me to look after the girls. That was a very hurtful period."

All of the tensions surrounding Kim Campbell's childhood seem to coalesce around a freak accident on a snowy toboggan hill in 1957. A hard fall on ice left Phyllis incapacitated. She couldn't get in or out of a chair and the girls had to help her get dressed in the morning. Her hip joint had been shattered and she would never again be able to walk without the aid of crutches or a cane.

According to Phyllis's sister Shirley McPhail — not quite an unbiased source — George was unsympathetic. McPhail alleges that George came home one night and told his wife he had been dancing with another woman. "She's not a hopeless cripple like you," he is quoted as saying.

The story may be suspect, but there's no doubt George did become involved with a young woman at around this time. Her name was Ginny, and she was not yet 21 — the generally accepted age of adulthood at that time. Phyllis apparently knew that George wanted to divorce her and marry Ginny. "George wanted to wait until she was 21 to marry Ginny," she says.

In her interview with Stephen Brunt, Phyllis said she asked George for a divorce repeatedly but he would not grant it. However, in her interview with Judy Steed, Phyllis suggests that George forced her out of the house even though she wanted to stay in the marriage until the girls were old enough to leave home.

"It was horrible in those days, for women," Phyllis is quoted as saying. "Whoever could drive the one out of the house got everything." Phyllis feared ending up "in a miserable boarding house in the east end, with George showering the girls with gifts and money and eventually destroying my relationship with them."

In the fall of 1959, Phyllis persuaded George to enroll the girls at St. Ann's Academy in Victoria, a Catholic boarding school. A month later, when the girls were safely installed, she left the house on 33rd Avenue never to return again.

She had a rendez-vous in England with Bill Vroom, a real estate agent who was also escaping from an unpleasant marriage. They planned to go sailing in the Caribbean.

According to Phyllis, George was taken by surprise. She left a letter for him to be mailed the day after she left. Allowing for the time it takes to deliver a letter, George must have spent a day or more without knowing what had happened to his wife. She claims he "phoned everybody, apparently panicked that I was gone. In a way, he didn't want me to go."

Phyllis married Vroom in London, England. She worked in a Red Cross clinic for a while, then they sailed a yacht to Portugal but ran out of money. From this point her story fades into obscurity. Phyllis seems to have wound up as a cook on rich people's yachts.

Phyllis's sudden disappearance was undoubtedly traumatic for Kim and Alix. Divorce was still rare in the 1950s. This was an era when "Leave It to Beaver" and "Father Knows Best" ruled prime time, purveying the myth of a perfect, always-happy, two-parent family. Single-parent families were stigmatized as "broken homes." But if Kim was hurt it didn't show. She remained her outgoing self and was popular enough at St. Ann's to win the title of Carnival Queen. The archivist for the Sisters of St. Ann's says Campbell was a hit in the classroom too.

"Her teacher has nothing but good to say about her whole attitude and conduct while she was here," says the sister, who doesn't want her name used. "And also her brilliance. She was an outstanding student. Her marks would verify that. She blended, she was really very sociable with everyone she met. Her teacher said she would brighten any classroom."

George Campbell has maintained a stoic silence since Phyllis went public with her allegations about him. "I don't think anybody has a right to know about my personal life," says Campbell, now in his 70s. "And I am resisting opening what I consider to be a closed book. It can't be reactivated. So I don't want to talk about it because I don't want to be in a position of debating what happened. I know that that can leave the impression in the eye of the beholder that Mr. Campbell doesn't want to talk because he feels guilty, which is not the case at all."

It's understandable that George would not want to endanger his daughter's image by getting into a mud-slinging match with his ex-wife in the national media. Nevertheless, the whole sad saga of what happened in the Campbell family 30 years ago has slid inexorably into the public domain. Some may object that the media are invading the privacy of Campbell's family, but the personal lives of prime ministers have always been scrutinized, and the only unusual thing in Kim Campbell's case is that there's so much interesting material. The early lives of Lester Pearson, John Diefenbaker, Joe Clark, or for that matter, Brian Mulroney simply don't compare when it comes to conflict and drama.

Kim has been thrust into the difficult role of defending her mother, who presumably could do further damage, without putting her father in a bad light. Phyllis suggests that Kim and Alix were alienated from their father, but it is George who has been making public appearances with Kim, not Phyllis. It was George who sat beside Kim on the stage of the Ottawa Civic Centre when she was elected Conservative leader. Kim touched on these delicate matters in her interview with Peter Newman.

> *She (Phyllis) was not, as some press people imply, some kind of flibbertigibbet who ran off to the Mediterranean," says Campbell. "My mother left a very difficult marriage, and the circumstances in which she wound up in Europe had nothing to do with any indifference to her children and had everything to do with powerlessness of women in those days. My mother was anything but uncaring and, in fact, a lot of what I am and a lot of my strengths, I owe to her. I had a very loving childhood. The breakup of my parents' marriage was very painful for me, and being on my own as a teenager was very painful, but it was not any indifference on the part of my mother that resulted in that separation.*

Studies have shown that children of divorced parents often suffer lifelong psychological repercussions, and often have difficulty forming stable relationships. But George Campbell believes the divorce made Kim more independent. "She's a tough girl. It didn't create any toughness or strength that wasn't already there. But it honed it."

Ralph White, who dated Kim in the years following the divorce, is not so sure. "Both Alix and Kim from outward appearances took it very well," says White. "Inwardly . . . that's hard to determine. But outwardly they took it well. Kim just threw herself into all sorts of activities at school and eventually became quite political.

"She was always ready to debate anyone on the issues. Basically the person you see today was an extension or development of those years and I guess one has to question whether she would have been that way with her mother or not. Perhaps she would have, maybe she wouldn't have."

Campbell's family were not church-goers but she did pick up a certain amount of religious instruction along the way, she told Peter Newman.

> *I went to a lot of different churches. I had a friend who went to the Pentecostal church and I went with her for a couple of years to Sunday School. I can still recite all the books of the Bible off by heart and sing all sorts of rousing hymns. When I went to St. Ann's, which was of course a convent school, it was in pre-Vatican II days. The nuns still wore habits, the mass was in Latin, and I got confirmed as an Anglican the year I was here, I suppose as a way of warding off*

the evil demons of the Papacy or whatever. But I have a lot of respect for the spiritual principles. I absorbed a lot of the ethic without the dogma. I guess I'm uneasy about organized religions because of the way they treat women. I've always had a skeptic's eye. I would never be dismissive of what people got from whatever form of worship they choose. We must all seek our own sources of spiritual support. At the end of the day I can lie to everybody but myself. I try to live in a way that makes it possible for me to face myself in the mirror, and when I say I would lie to everybody I don't mean that I do. I mean that that's really where it all comes back to.

CHAPTER 3

KIM DEFINES HERSELF

In his interesting book *Reading Kim Right*, Frank Davey whips up a virtual hurricane of significance around the fact of Kim having renamed herself at age 12. It's a delight to see a cultivated mind at play. Davey says the act of self-naming "has been loaded with meaning throughout human history" and draws links between Campbell and many legendary figures from Venus to Davey Crockett. His discussion is fascinating but he seems to overlook the possibility that Kim simply didn't like her original name, Avril. Who can blame her? The name was unusual in a way that displeased her and people had difficulty pronouncing it.

With her mother gone there was no one to stop her from calling herself what she wanted. Also, there was the anger and the trauma at having been abandoned. Rejecting the name that her absent mother had given her may have been a kind of symbolic retaliation. Then again, it's worth remembering that there was something of a tradition for name changes in the family. Her mother had been christened Phyllis but called herself Lissa. Her father was named George but adopted the name Paul at his wife's insistence, until she eloped whereupon he became George once again.

Campbell seems to have compensated for private unhappiness by throwing herself into the life of the group. Her high school career is one of frenetic activity. She led hootenannies, published poetry, partied (her father apparently made a point of throwing his house open for the purpose) and won awards for academic achievement.

George Campbell continued his relationship with the young Ginny and finally married her when Kim was in grade eleven. Kim and Alix now had a stepmother who was barely older than they were. As one family friend put it, a stranger who saw them sitting together would have thought they were three sisters.

"You could tell there was a little bit of tension," Ralph White recalls. "I guess in those days divorce was not a common thing and I don't think people really felt that comfortable with it and certainly it was tough on Kim and Alix . . . because of Ginny."

Another family friend says that George expected Ginny to exercise discipline over his daughters. "If you are George with two young daughters who are coming in late at night, how do you get your young wife to control them?"

Meanwhile there was tension between Kim and Alix, as reported by Phil Rankin who knew Alix well. It would not be surprising if an older daughter were annoyed at being constantly outshone by a younger sister, and the problem was reinforced by their father's favoritism.

"Kim was the apple of her daddy's eye and Alix was the naughty one," says Rankin. "There was a sibling kind of rivalry between them. Alix fooled around with the boys and Kim sat up in her room and dreamed of being a Rhodes scholar or whatever she dreamed about and one was a good girl, one was a bad girl."

White totally rejects Rankin's interpretation. "He doesn't know where the hell he's coming from," says White.

White is one of the more sympathetic figures in the Campbell story. He comes across as sincere, good-natured, down-to-earth. He remembers taking Kim out for dinner, going to Elvis Presley movies, going on double-dates with Alix and her boyfriend, and even writing songs with Kim.

"We played them on the piano and we had a great plan of publishing all these songs because we thought they were much better than anything that was being produced on the radio at that time.

"I guess Paul Anka had made his presence known and we thought, well, jeez, these songs are every bit as good as anything that Paul Anka's doing. I've often wondered what she's done with them. It would be interesting to get them out."

It all sounds rather carefree, but White recalls another side of the story.

"You know, like, the cold war was still on. They were still building bomb shelters, for chrissake. You know, there was the Kennedy assassination and just a lot of things that drove a lot of people together. When I look at my kids, the groups that they went with didn't seem to be as intense as the groups that we went with. I still see a lot of these people. We still get away for skiing trips. I don't know if my kids will be as close to their friends as I was to mine. I think it goes back to that particular time in history. Like there was a lot of nervousness and I think getting together was a kind of safety net."

Did Campbell realize then that she had some special mission or destiny?

"She made comments about it," says White. "Whether they were a Freudian slip or not is hard to determine but she did say she wanted to be the secretary-general of the United Nations. Some people, some of her girlfriends, said that she thought she wanted to be prime minister."

White said he still sees Campbell occasionally. "My wife and I were involved with the science centre which was getting some government grants so there were some occasions where, you know, I went out for dinner with her (Campbell) with regards to Science World and a few other things. I mean she's really interested in education and more or less, I guess, helping people in the province."

He speaks admiringly of her ambition to be prime minister, saying he would never aspire to the job himself. "Kim, she's single, she's got no baggage, she'll really get into it. She's single, she's got no family, I think she would give it a real good shot. Of course the big thing is, can she do anything or is she powerless to do anything once she's there? I haven't talked to any prime ministers, I don't know what happens when you get there. It's kind of a mystery to most of us, I guess."

He bristles at the suggestion that Campbell is elitist. "She was always reaching out to meet other people. She really got involved in debating issues with people that perhaps our group wouldn't associate with. But she could always see a little bit further than us. It's kind of hard to explain. We were so comfortable with each other but Kim was reaching out a little bit further all the time."

In grade 12 Campbell was elected class president, an event unusual enough to be reported in the *Vancouver Sun.*

> *A pretty strawberry blonde who thought some new ideas were needed at Prince of Wales High School ended up making history there.*
>
> *Freckle-faced Kim Campbell, 16, of 2707 West Thirty-third has been elected first girl president of the student council in the school's 43 years.*
>
> *"I thought it was time to try some new ideas and get a girl elected," she said. Kim beat two male opponents capturing more than 50 per cent of the vote of the 100 students.*
>
> *But she said charm had nothing to do with winning. "We convinced them I can do a good job," she said. "I may not do a better job than in the past but it will be different."*
>
> *Five feet four inches Kim said she has no fear about getting cooperation from other members of the council.*
>
> *"There are some pretty big boys on it but I'll have a gavel," she said.*

At the outset of her term as school president, Campbell reorganized the house system at Prince of Wales, then, writing in the school newspaper, declared the operation a great success.

She urged students to participate in intramural activities, but warned them not to forget their studies: "There is no time like the present to start hitting those books. Time passes — will you?"

Campbell's final message as class president is not a bad piece of writing. It avoids clichés, does not become saccharine and probably portrays the students' state of mind quite accurately.

> *As the year draws to a close, you probably are looking forward to your holidays — the trips you're going to take, the fortune you're going to earn, the gorgeous tan you'll acquire, and all the romances you'll have. Or perhaps you're wondering just how you're going to pass all your (ugh) exams. For grads, these last few days are both happy and sad. While we are looking forward to summer and whatever follows, we can't help feeling a little regret that we won't be returning to good old P.W. in the fall. (or will we?)*

Prince of Wales must have been an innovative school. The students not only had a newspaper but also a radio station. They also published collections of poetry, including some of Campbell's.

The "Status Quo"

Must I stand by and watch my world be destroyed
I cannot bear to face that ominous threat
To the ideals of beauty and justice that I love;
For I cannot feel the hatreds that some feel,
And I cannot crush another human soul!
In my dead world, ten billion men are walking,
But within the mounds of human flesh and blood
Are ugly loveless souls
Who work and seek to feed a deity of destruction
But cannot soothe the hunger of a child.

"Canada"

The call of a wild goose
Breaks the stillness of a northern sky:
"CANADA! CANADA!"
At the ocean's edge whispering waves
Lap tenderly at the shore:
"CANADA! CANADA!"
High above the plain a small boy
Sends out his echoing cry:
"CANADA! CANADA!"
A mass of steel wheels in a factory
Booms out its productive roar:
"CANADA! CANADA!"
Below tall buildings busy footsteps
Beat down upon the street:
"CANADA! CANADA!"
Within my breast throbs
One pulsating beat:
"CANADA! CANADA!"

CHAPTER

4

A CUDDLY CANDIDATE

The University of British Columbia campus is perched beside high cliffs that overlook the ocean. A steeply descending path leads to Wreck Beach, a magnificent swimming spot strewn with driftwood. Kim was only 17 when she arrived on the campus where she would meet her first husband and form her basic philosophy.

It was here that she encountered the ideas of Edmund Burke, the eighteenth-century British writer and statesman who she has often cited as a major influence in her intellectual development. It's an unusual choice in heroes. Certainly Campbell can't be accused of going with the fads of her time. Many people of that time were inspired by John Kennedy, Che Gueverra or Martin Luther King. But Edmund Burke?

In the search for clues about Campbell's intellectual orientation it may be worth pausing over the Burke connection.

Burke was no ivory tower philosopher. He served in the House of Commons and held several important jobs in the British government. He was not an innovator but made his reputation by defending the aristocratic world in which he lived. He condemned the French Revolution and correctly predicted the terror that came in its wake. Burke had a dim view of human nature and considered the average man incapable of solving problems in a rational manner. He spoke for the English ruling class and generally fought to preserve the established order of things. Burkean scholar Frank O'Gorman says that Burke was really not a philosopher at all. "He was essentially a practical politician and a propagandist rather than a thinker with a systematic philosophy to expound."

The Burkean approach sounds remarkably similar to the neo-conservatism of the 1980s and '90s. Like Burke, Campbell has no systematic philosophy, but develops her arguments in response to specific situations as they occur. This is what makes her hard to categorize.

Adaptable though he was, Burke probably would have raised his eyebrows at Campbell's campaign for the presidency of the UBC Frosh Society. She didn't shy away from using her sex appeal as a campaign weapon. Her campaign slogan was "more cuddly." Her picture appeared in the student newspaper six times in her first year on campus. Her blue eyes dazzle even in black and white.

One photograph shows her eyeing an apparently naked engineer at her 18th birthday party.

The engineer is holding a sign which says "18 Now You're UNRESTRICTED." The man has bare shoulders and legs. He may have been wearing something behind the sign, just as Kim may have been wearing something in her famous bare-shoulders picture years later. Who knows?

University students are expected to get involved in dumb escapades, and Campbell seems to have enjoyed a few. Consider this challenge issued to fellow student councillors in the *Ubyssey*, the student newspaper, on November 6, 1964.

> *Frosh president Kim Campbell takes on the undergraduate society presidents in a buggy race today.*
> *Teams made up of an undergrad president and a partner will navigate an obstacle course down the Main Mall.*
> *One member will push and the other ride. The riding baby must eat a bowl of pablum at the end of the course, then dismount to push his partner through the return trip.*
> *Both members of each team will be dressed in diapers. Miss Campbell said prizes will be announced after the contest.*
> *Kim challenged the presidents to the race at Monday's council meeting.*

It's not clear whether the challenge was accepted. Campbell's performance as frosh president got generally favorable reviews. Some of the comments on her regime were quoted in the *Ubyssey*. The suggestive nature of the comments as they were placed in the student newspaper is probably not accidental:

> *She seems a lot more emphatic than the boys.*
> *Women are just the same.*
> *She bounces around a lot.*
> *I think it's an indication of the shape of things to come.*

Campbell's earliest and possibly her only published essay appears in the *Ubyssey* of November 9, 1965. The topic is relations between the sexes. Her article is juxtaposed with another by one John Kelsey. The debate is clearly intended as a joke, with both sides taking outrageous positions.

Kelsey says that modern man must "insert these screaming vixen who would frillify the world and emasculate us all into their proper roles: pregnant, barefoot and in the kitchen. He must beat them into submission, showing no quarter, allowing no favor."

The photograph shows a smiling Kim Campbell head-to-head with her glowering adversary, whose lighted cigarette is just a few inches from her nose.

> *What's all this garbage about women trying to dominate the world. Women ought to and women do. The old platitude*

about a woman behind every man is no joke. But now is the time for women to stop letting men take the credit for what we are accomplishing.

For millions of years women have catered to the male ego, only to produce a breed of male with utter delusions of grandeur and, get this, the notion that women are the weaker sex.

Not that women have always objected. Occasionally, it has been to the decided advantage of women to appear weak and helpless.

However, since it is becoming more and more difficult to maintain this illusion, perhaps women ought to scrap it entirely and avoid hypocrisy.

Women are not only as good as men in most fields they are better. We must concede men's superiority in a few areas. For example, men are said to make better chefs than women.

If more men could be induced to stand over hot stoves, push vacuums and wash dishes it would enable women to devote themselves to the important business of running the world for which they are so well suited.

In fact, women have a moral duty to save the world from the terrible mess that men have made of it. Women have waited patiently for the right time to assert themselves openly.

> *Opposition such as emanates from the nitwit above (referring to Kelsey's column) proves the time is now. Not that men haven't tried to do their best. But if they can't keep things straight after a million years, how long do we wait?*
> *After all fellas, "Namo dat quod non habet," "You can't give what you haven't got." Rise women, let's tidy up the world and start running it properly.*

Quoting Latin proverbs is another Campbell habit that surfaces later. As a cabinet minister in Ottawa she liked to baffle reporters with Latin quips.

CHAPTER 5

TUZIE

The Canadian society into which Campbell graduated in 1969 was seething with social change. Canada's baby-boom generation was coming of age. Born in the optimism that followed the war, baby-boomers had none of the humility that comes from economic hardship. Instead of being grateful for their affluence, many of them were alienated by the materialistic, status-seeking society their parents had created.

Vancouver was a counter-culture Mecca teeming with hippies, American draft-dodgers and activists of every stripe. One of the products of this ferment was Greenpeace, which eventually became the world's biggest environmental group. Vancouver's biggest hippie neighborhood was Kitsilano, right next to Kerrisdale where the Campbell family lived.

Many Vancouver residents were not happy with all the "subversive" activity. Their chief spokesman was Mayor Tom Campbell. His comment on the longhairs constantly demonstrating in front of the court house fountain was: "The scum always rises to the surface." Tom's no relation to Kim but there's a certain political affinity. When Kim Campbell ran for the Vancouver School Board, later, she did so under the banner of the Non-Partisan Association, the same party that Tom Campbell represented during his years as mayor.

Campbell does not seem to have identified with the counter-culture. There is no hint of her being involved in any of the protests or demonstrations which were so frequent in those days. She has admitted trying marijuana, adding, "And I inhaled the smoke." But she later said she didn't like it and didn't think it should be legalized. She even denied that she had broken the law, causing some consternation in legal circles.

Charlotte Gray says Campbell was "more mature than many of her long-haired peers" and "kept her distance from what she regarded as 'trendy' student radicalism."

After a term as vice-president of the Alma Mater Society (student council), Campbell dropped out of student politics.

University days are prime time for romance and broken hearts. Kim Campbell had all the attributes for success in the dating game — looks, intelligence and confidence. It seems safe to assume that she would have had the pick of the crop of young men. But Campbell has never behaved in conventional fashion and she demonstrated her unusual tastes by going for a plump, married, middle-aged mathematics professor with frizzy hair.

Campbell met Nathan Divinsky through a group that produced Gilbert and Sullivan operettas on campus. She was 20 and he was 45, the father of three teen-aged daughters. "In a strange twist of fate, or an act of unconscious repetition, Kim was about the same age as Ginny in relation to her father when she started seeing Tuzie," comments Judy Steed.

Known to his friends as Tuzie, Divinsky was a colorful character from a Jewish family, and had been raised in the north end of Winnipeg. He had at one time belonged to the Co-operative Commonwealth Federation, forerunner to the New Democratic Party. By the time Campbell met him the needle on his political compass had swung around 180 degrees and he was known for his outrageously right-wing views. He liked to defend Britain's rigid class system, and was not embarrassed about seeking the life of luxury with a strong accent on good food and drink.

"Tuzie's very reactionary and elitist," said a fellow UBC professor Fritz Bowers. "Tuzie wouldn't admit it but he thinks the important thing is to look after the interests of the intelligentsia, the people who lead society."

Divinsky and Campbell first lived together in the summer of 1969 at Eugene, Oregon according to a story in *Maclean's* by Mary Janigan and E. Kaye Fulton. Divinsky was teaching summer courses at the University of Oregon, and Campbell enrolled in a political science course there — oddly enough, on revolution. While many of her peers were trying to make revolution, she was taking a course in it.

The couple shared a furnished apartment in a small complex with a swimming pool. They partied with Divinsky's faculty colleagues, taking the male and female leads in impromptu performances of Gilbert and Sullivan operettas. It was not common in those days for professors and students to live together and there were some raised eyebrows. *Maclean's* quotes one Betty Niven who knew the couple in Oregon. "I noticed during those times with Tuzie that she (Campbell) was very self-confident and had a lot of presence. After all, they were not married yet. Nobody was looking down their nose, but there were not a lot of people in that situation."

Much has been made of Divinsky's skill in chess. Writing in *Vancouver Magazine*, Peter Newman describes him as "an internationally renowned chess expert." But veterans of the Canadian chess scene say he never made it past the intermediate level. They describe him as the Don Cherry of Canadian chess, a reference to the hockey commentator who is known more for bluster than finesse.

Divinsky also had a knack for dealing with money. He and Campbell were founding investors in Jalm Holdings Ltd., owner of

Bridges Restaurant on Granville Island, which became immensely successful. Campbell's share in Jalm Holdings eventually helped to make her financially secure.

Everyone who knows Campbell agrees that Divinsky had a profound influence on her. "He was a father to her, a friend to her, a scholar to her," says Shirley McPhail, Campbell's aunt. Janigan and Fulton say in *Maclean's* that "Divinsky's impact upon her was more profound than Campbell today acknowledges."

Charlotte Gray even goes so far as to suggest in *Saturday Night* that Divinsky was "Campbell's Svengali" — an intriguing allusion. Svengali is the evil genius in George du Maurier's 1895 novel *Trilby*. He uses his hypnotic powers to transform an untalented young woman, Trilby, into a great singer. One hopes the analogy doesn't fit too closely, given the novel's tragic ending. Svengali dies of a heart attack during one of Trilby's concerts, and without his mysterious, hypnotic support, she utterly loses her ability to sing.

Not surprisingly for a person with a sizable ego, Campbell rejects the suggestions that Divinsky made her who she is.

"It's not true that he was my Svengali," she told Peter Newman. "I had as powerful an influence on him as he had on me. There were lots of things I learned about in the course of that relationship, but the same is true in reverse. He was the first man I ever felt really comfortable with. He was completely unthreatened and very confident in himself. We had some very good years together."

Even if he didn't have any hypnotic influence, Divinsky probably had a lot of useful advice for Campbell as she contemplated what to do with her life. He was something of a wheeler-dealer in the academic world with interests ranging far beyond his discipline. He knew how the system worked, and had some influence in it. He was UBC's assistant dean of sciences and sat on one of the awards selection committees at the Canada Council, the federal agency which supports the arts and social sciences.

By an odd coincidence, Campbell applied for a Canada Council fellowship in 1969, the same year that she began living with Divinsky. What's even more surprising is that she got the scholarship. Campbell had only her B.A., not her M.A., yet she was given approval to study at the London School of Economics, at the doctoral level, all expenses paid by the Canadian taxpayers. The Canada Council has confirmed that Nathan Divinsky sat on one of the council's awards selection committees at the time that Campbell's grant was approved. This raises the question of whether she won the grant on merit alone, or thanks to her "connection."

Campbell's application for the Canada Council fellowship, dated December 5, 1969, has been faithfully safeguarded in the Public Archives. In it, she says she contemplates a career "teaching university" and requests financial assistance to pursue doctoral studies for a

12-month period beginning August, 1970. She says her doctoral thesis topic will likely be "a research application of an empirical theory to some aspect of international relations."

There's a space on the application form where the candidates are asked to "outline as definitely as possible" their proposed program of research.

Campbell replies, "I shall be concerned with reading broadly in, and preparing to write comprehensive examinations in International Relations Theory, Methodology, and Comparative government. Most likely I shall want to continue my work in Southeast Asian politics and I would like, if possible, to do some work in Canadian government. I see my work in comparative government and area studies as providing a basis for the application of general theories of international political behavior."

It's hard to overlook the fuzziness of this statement. The territory that Campbell proposes to explore is vast. Her statement could include almost anything in the world having to do with government or politics.

It's unusual to take on studies at the doctoral level without first having completed a Master's Degree. Some people skip the intermediate step but it's rare. Anyway, Campbell does not propose to skip her Master's; rather, she promises it will be done imminently. It's possible that staff at the Canada Council were misled by a letter they received just before the application was approved.

The University of British Columbia
Department of Political Science
Vancouver 8
Canada
August 12, 1970

Mr. Jules Pelletier
Chief of Awards Service
Canada Council
140 Wellington Street
Ottawa 4 Ontario
Dear Sir:

I am writing regarding Miss Avril P.D. Campbell (W 70 2300) who is finishing a M.A. degree at U.B.C. and who will be attending the London School of Economics in the fall under the financial auspices of the Canada Council. She completed her course work in May (with first class standing in both her seminars), and she is presently completing her M.A. essay which we expect will be finished by the time she departs for England on September 14.

Sincerely,
(signed)
Jean A. Laponce
Acting Head

Evidently the Canada Council took this letter to mean that Campbell's Master's degree was in the bag. Certainly that is the tone of the letter. It's baffling that the acting head of the UBC political science department would make such a confident prediction that the thesis would be finished on September 14, considering that it never was finished.

Five days after the Canada Council received the persuasive letter quoted above, they sent her a cheque for $1,894.00 to cover air fare to London, tuition at the LSE, and initial living expenses in London.

It's also puzzling that Campbell was admitted to doctoral studies at the LSE without having completed her Master's degree. An LSE admissions official said in an interview that the school requires students wishing to conduct studies at the doctoral level to have completed their Master's. But policies might have been different in the 1970s, the official added.

CHAPTER 6

THE UNFINISHED THESIS

The London School of Economics is housed in a nondescript gray building on Houghton Street, not far from Fleet Street, surrounded by hustling humanity, dust and exhaust. It lacks the rolling lawns, shaded walks, and ivied courtyards normally associated with havens of higher learning. The LSE has always been close to the nitty gritty of real life. Many of its students have gone on to powerful positions in governments of the Commonwealth.

It's ironic that Campbell wanted to study at the LSE, since it is closely associated with socialist currents to which she normally seems allergic. The school was founded by Sidney and Beatrice Webb of the Fabian Society, a group of British intellectuals who basically invented the modern Welfare State. Their ideas have taken a lot of abuse over the past few decades, but as Anne Fremantle writes in her history of the Fabians, they saw the

Welfare State "as the only possible preventative against, and alternative to, the Police State."

Campbell studied at the London School of Economics from 1970 to 1974, and this stint has contributed to her reputation as a brilliant intellectual.

At some point in her first year or two at London she established a rapport with a professor named Leonard Schapiro, who taught Soviet studies. She then decided to focus her research on Soviet issues although she had not mentioned this topic in her initial grant application.

Maclean's writers, Janigan and Fulton, say that Campbell's "studies at LSE reinforced her conservative views. Her doctoral supervisor was Leonard Schapiro, a brilliant Sovietologist who shepherded his students on a three-month tour of the Soviet Union. Campbell emerged from his influence with a loathing for leftist dogma — and a profound respect for the law."

Schapiro became a valuable ally. He countersigned the regular progress reports which Campbell was required to send the Canada Council as a condition of funding. These reports are extremely brief, each one consisting of only a few words. They look as if they were scrawled in a hurry and some words are actually illegible — Schapiro was evidently quite old — but they convey the impression that he liked her very much and thought her an outstanding student.

On January 1, 1973 Campbell wrote the Canada Council to announce her doctoral thesis topic: The Role of Political Socialization in Legitimizing Political Change in the USSR — the case of De-Stalinization. "I have chosen this topic because I am interested in the problem of political socialization in highly centralized or 'totalitarian' societies," she says.

> *The current theory in the area of political socialization derives from the study of pluralistic societies. The underlying assumption of this theory is that socialization has a direct bearing on the political actions of individuals and therefore on the political complexion of the society. Since there are a variety of roles individuals may play it then becomes interesting to study how these roles develop. However, in trying to examine the process of political socialization in the Soviet Union we find that we cannot make the same assumptions about the outcome of the socialization process. We require, then, what David Easton has called "a political theory of political socialization" which would explain the role of political socialization in the Soviet Union before we can understand its significance in the Soviet context. Therefore, I am trying to examine the role that socialization plays in a highly centralized polity such as the Soviet Union. In particular, I am interested in the implications of a highly centralized, rigidly orthodox system of socialization. Can it succeed? Is it efficient? In particular, how does such a system react to an "about face" in policy without compromising its own legitimacy? How does it legit-*

imize social change? I am examining the problem in the context of de-Stalinization which I consider to be a fundamental change of policy and a useful case for study. I believe the result will be a useful contribution to the theory of political socialization.

All this could probably be reduced to three or four sentences of plain English but in the end she really did have a hot topic. She understood that the Soviet totalitarian apparatus was beginning to crumble. She wondered whether the Kremlin would be able to move to a more open system without losing control. An excellent question, to which history has now provided the answer (no).

Campbell's Soviet studies were capped in early 1972 with a three-month tour behind the Iron Curtain, as it was then known. Travel in the Soviet Union at that time was generally arranged by Intourist, a state agency. It provided everything in the finest style that the creaking Soviet bureaucracy could deliver. Jeff Sallot of the *Globe and Mail* says she visited Moscow, Samarkand, Tashkent, Alma Ata, Kiev, Odessa and Riga, "finishing the journey with a midnight toast of Tang orange drink with some fellow Canadians during the blazing white nights in Leningrad."

Campbell and Divinsky were married in London later that year. He was on a year's sabbatical leave and they spent a lot of time going to the theatre. In 1973 Divinsky had to return to Vancouver since his sabbatical was over. Campbell went with him even though she had a year to go in her doctoral program at the LSE. She applied to get her Canada Council funding extended once again even though she was no longer a registered student at the school.

Schapiro helped out once again, sending the Canada Council a note saying, "I am fully satisfied that Miss Campbell can adequately complete her Ph.D. with the resources available to her in Vancouver." The Canada Council accepted these assurances, and dished out money to support Campbell one more year. Schapiro's last progress report, dated September 30, 1974, states: "In my view the awardholder is progressing satisfactorily in her current program and is expected to complete it by the end of the year."

Schapiro's expectations — and those of the Canada Council — turned out to be overly optimistic. Two years later, the council was still waiting.

28 February, 1976
Miss Avril P.D. Campbell
5689 McMaster Rd.
Vancouver, B.C.
V6T 1K1

Dear Miss Campbell:
Re: Doctoral Fellowship W70-2300 — W71-4401 — W72-3567 and W73-2951

In looking over our files we note that the period of your award from the Canada Council ended some time ago. We should like to remind you that one of the conditions under which awards are granted is that a final report be submitted to the Council after the period for which the grant is authorized. Even though your entire program may not yet be completed we should appreciate hearing from you in the near future as the Council has to be in a position to account annually for its awards. Will you therefore let us know how your work progressed and tell us of any specific accomplishments which you achieved? Any information which you may like to send later will always be welcome.

We shall look forward to receiving this information soon, unless of course you have just recently submitted a report which we had not received before this date of writing.

Yours sincerely,
Norman Lamont
Chief, Fellowship Section
Humanities and Social Sciences Division

The letter was evidently not answered, since Lamont sent Campbell an identical missive some nine months later, on October 15. Finally, Campbell replied as follows:

Oct. 25, 1976
Mr. Norman Lamont,
Awards Service,
The Canada Council
151 Sparks Street,
Ottawa, Ontario K1P 5V8

Dear Mr. Lamont,
Re: Doctoral Fellowships W702300, W714401, W72 3567 & W732951.

I am happy to report that completion of my doctoral dissertation is now in sight. Since January, 1975, I have been employed in various capacities by the Department of Political Science at the University of British Columbia. Specifically, I have been engaged as a sessional lecturer — part time, Jan. - April, 1975; a visiting lecturer — full time, July 1975 - July 1976; and a sessional lecturer — part time, September 1976 - April, 1977.

I had hoped to submit my thesis this past summer, but was unable to meet the deadline.

In May and June of this year I spent six weeks in London in order to confer with my thesis supervisor, Professor Schapiro. I now believe I shall be able to submit and defend my thesis during the summer of 1977.

I apologize for being so uncommunicative. I continue to be very grateful for the generous support of the Council during my years of graduate study.

Yours truly,
(signed)
Ms Avril P.D. Campbell

The Canada Council finally gave up pursuing Campbell about her thesis which was never finished. But the lack of academic credentials would continue to haunt her in Canada. If she really was planning on a career teaching at the university level, as she had said in her initial grant application, she was out of luck. Anyone contemplating a tenured position at a Canadian university must have a doctorate.

Campbell survived for several years on short-term teaching jobs, apparently while still working on her thesis, or at least claiming to. But she was in an unsustainable position. Sessional jobs are generally given to scholars completing a thesis, but they are not renewed indefinitely. Philip Resnick, professor of political science at UBC, suggests that Campbell ran out of time. "It was for her to get those credentials and she didn't," he says. "With all due respect to her, she would have had to have that degree finished . . . or close to it."

Campbell was bitter about her inability to get a university job and later suggested her problems were due to anti-female discrimination, a claim that has been picked up in numerous articles. Charlotte Gray says Campbell "applied for a political science professorship at Simon Fraser University, and was outraged to be told that 'not only had they hired an American man but they'd even lost my resume.'"

Peter Newman says Campbell was "denied a tenure track position by administrations . . . that seemed to regard political science as a man's discipline." In a speech to the Women in the Media Conference in November 1992, Campbell said "I started my working life as an academic. Academia, I might add, is the last great bastion of sexism in this country. It is unbelievable, unbelievable."

Unable to continue at UBC, Campbell got a part-time job at the Langara College, a branch of the Vancouver Community College. It's a respected local school, but it's not a degree-granting university.

Ralph Toren was head of the college's political science department when Campbell applied for a job there. He hired her on a part-time basis and admits it was a controversial decision within the school.

"She just had a B.A., not an M.A.," he said. "The college policy was M.A. or equivalent and we thought she'd done a couple of years on her Ph.D. and that was equivalent to an M.A. And also UBC thought she was capable of teaching second-year or third-year courses."

Toren says there was an opening for a full-time job, but he couldn't give it to Campbell because another candidate had a doctorate. Yet he speaks highly of her.

"As soon as she was elected (Member of Parliament) I thought that she'd be going places. She handled herself well. You know, she's got a friendly personality and a lot of self-confidence. It was obvious that she was very ambitious. If she'd got the steady job, she'd be the president of the college here now, I think."

Despite all her personality and confidence, Campbell had run out of options in the academic world. She could not get a steady job. She had hit a dead end. The average person would have thrown up her hands in despair but that's not Campbell's style.

CHAPTER 7

THE COMEBACK

Like a general who is cornered, Campbell found her fighting spirit in 1980. The prospect of unemployment no doubt focused her mind. Those now-or-never insights come to everyone from time to time, but not everyone has the capacity to carry through. She did.

To switch metaphors, it was almost like a caterpillar changing into a butterfly. Within the space of three years she would have a new job, a new home, a new public identity and a new marital status.

Her actions at this point look like they were consciously planned with a clear objective, which was to establish herself in a political career. She had Divinsky's help in drawing up the strategy but when it had been successfully executed he found to his surprise there was no place left for him.

It was a two-track operation — track one was enrolling in law school to get some credentials; track two was getting hands-on experience and public exposure by entering local politics.

Divinsky had served several terms on the Vancouver School Board, including one term as chairman, a position that paid some $6,000 a year. He had connections in the Non-Partisan Association (NPA), which was influential in Vancouver politics and had controlled the school board for many years. Rather than seeking another term on school board, Divinsky ran for city council, leaving the way clear for Campbell to run for the board.

The Vancouver School Board was not an insignificant operation. It had a budget of around $150 million and wide powers over schools serving more than 50,000 students.

School boards are not usually hotbeds of political excitement, but these were unusual times in British Columbia. The Social Credit government of Bill Bennett had embarked on a major campaign to cut the budget and the education system had been selected as a prime target. School boards across the province were ordered to cut costs. Especially hard hit were programs requiring special resources such as French immersion, music, drama and science. Parents and teachers were up in arms.

"It was fireworks," recalls Carol Volkart who covered education for the *Vancouver Sun* at the time. "There was a lot of tension and excitement and you never knew what was going to happen. Sometimes they (the trustees) would hold their meetings in the schools and whoever was particularly furious would come and there'd be really ugly scenes."

Both Campbell and Divinsky won their seats in the municipal elections. Campbell was able to drop her part-time job teaching at Langara College.

Campbell and Divinsky both represented the Non-Partisan Association which, despite its name, was anything but non-partisan. It had been founded in 1937 to combat the socialists of the CCF and gradually evolved into a Social Credit farm team. It was closely linked to the Vancouver business community and one of its main interests was keeping education taxes down. Opposing the NPA on every front was the left-leaning Committee of Progressive Electors (COPE). In their battle with COPE the NPA trustees were faced with a dilemma — they were supposed to be protecting the school system, yet they were also committed (unofficially) to protecting the provincial government.

"It was a very torn thing always," says Volkart. "Some (of the NPA councillors) would be really strongly committed to the Social Credit government's agenda. Others would see what impact it was having on the schools and what it meant, the cuts they were going to have to make, so they were wavering."

Phil Rankin, who served as a trustee for COPE, describes the NPA as a two-issue party: "No more taxing residential property owners, no more raising school taxes. And occasionally, 'We have to do something about gifted education.' Once in a while they got on to something like gender or something that they thought sounded OK but they never did anything. They were really a do-nothing group."

School board meetings tended to be fractious. "It was just passionate hatred (between the two sides)," says Volkart. The minutes in the school board archives are punctuated with remarks such as Campbell's retort, "Put a can in it, Rankin." But there were lighter moments too, as when the council unanimously voted to phase out junk food in the school cafeterias. Campbell agreed there was no need for soft drinks and commercially packaged high-fat, high-salt and high-sugar foods, but balked at extending the ban to foods containing white flour and white rice. "We'll all be eating Wheat Berries," said Campbell. "I can't see it — and I'm quite a healthy eater, known to eat alfalfa sprouts from time to time. I'm not advocating plastic bread."

The mood became more bitter as the budget-cutting process advanced. At a public meeting in September, Campbell drew hisses from an audience of about 750 with her suggestion that teachers should give up a day's pay to help ease the school board's financial problems. News reports don't say whether she volunteered to sacrifice some of her pay as well.

CHAPTER 8

DIVORCE

Campbell's political career was getting under way, but her marriage with Divinsky was breaking down. She has never spoken about the reasons for the split with Divinsky, but it may not be such a big mystery since even his friends describe him as an overbearing personality.

Campbell's mother Lissa Vroom (formerly Phyllis Cook) doesn't mince her words about Divinsky. "I found him rude and pushy. I was surprised Kim was attracted to him. He's quite brilliant. But that doesn't make people likable."

According to Stephen Brunt, Divinsky refused to join in Christmas carols when he came to Port Alberni for Christmas one year. "He sat there like an anthropologist watching the natives at their curious rites," said Vroom. "I never warmed to him at all."

Vroom suggests the marriage might have worked if Campbell had had a baby. "She planned a family and it didn't happen," said Vroom. "I know that was in 1978 because that was the last thing that Bill (Vroom, her second husband with whom she had lived in Europe when Kim was 12) said to me about Kimmy. He was in the hospital having the heart surgery that he died of. Kimmy had been in visiting him and telling all the old men in the hospital about this baby she was going to have if she could manage it."

There may be another explanation for the drifting apart. Campbell had been attracted to Divinsky because she felt she could learn from him. But after nine years it may be there was no more to learn. She may even have come to see him as a political liability given his antics on Vancouver City Council.

Judy Lindsay, the *Sun's* city hall reporter, described Divinsky as "city council's clown alderman." She added, "Whether the debate needs it or not, he usually supplies the comic relief."

Divinsky's curious habits included things like conspicuously requesting the mayor's leave to munch on an apple, and working out a contract bridge problem during intense debate.

Among Divinsky's memorable lines at council: "We should kiss the feet of developers" and "Let's not look down our noses at greed and profit."

"His speeches on behalf of developers and the free enterprise system may be to the point, but they are couched in such General Bullmoose terms that they probably hurt more than help," commented Lindsay. "What bombs is his professorial style."

Divinsky generated more controversy when, in a speech to the UBC Progressive Conservative Club, he criticized pregnant single women who decide to keep their baby rather than put it up for adoption. "No one asked her to uncross her legs," he said.

"Women who run away from their husbands, where the husband is the breadwinner of the family, should not get public assistance," he added. "They should never have left their husbands in the first place."

His speech was a hit with the mainly male audience which applauded and cheered, but women's groups were outraged when they heard about it.

The *Sun* picked up key quotes from the *Ubyssey. Sun* columnist Linda Hossie attacked Divinsky mercilessly, saying he was "blind to his own sexism."

It's curious that a self-declared feminist like Campbell could have co-existed with an unapologetic chauvinist like Divinsky for nine years. But they split in 1982 and were divorced in 1983. It appears that Campbell was the one who left, while Divinsky was devastated. Friends recall getting anguished late-night telephone calls from him at the time.

She claimed later to have suffered greatly over the separation. "It was very, very traumatic for me. I felt a great sense of failure."

But the upheaval in her home life didn't prevent her from running for a second term on the school board, maintaining her studies at law school and organizing the annual law school gala show. Indeed, she seemed positively upbeat when interviewed for a profile by Carol Volkart a few months after the divorce.

One of her problems, she told Volkart, was being blessed with so many natural talents "by virtue of my genes" that it had been hard for her to decide what to do with her life. Besides music, dancing, and her academic ability, she claimed a talent for writing dialogue that she'd like to use to write plays.

She posed for a photograph with the deely bobbers that she wore to her weekly "beer-ups" with fellow law students. Deely-bobbers are wire antennae with balls at the ends, worn on the head, which wobble and bounce when a person moves. Campbell confessed she had "a very strong silly side."

Campbell was evidently not suffering financially, since she received Volkart in a rented condominium with a spectacular view of False Creek.

How could a law student earning $6,000 a year as chairman of the school board afford a condo with a view in the heart of Vancouver? She probably had Divinsky to thank. Her shares in Jalm Holdings had sharply increased in value and so had the house they jointly owned, which was now being sold. These assets, together with her excellent earning prospects as an articling student with Ladner Downs would have provided collateral for a substantial bank loan or mortgage.

In her interview with Volkart, Campbell talked about the possibility of a political career.

"I don't know whether I'm going to go any farther in politics or not. But I'm certainly not going to unless I feel a genuine interest in the issues that belong to a certain level of government.

"Maybe I will be interested in running for city council or the legislature or Parliament. But I see myself as someone who cares about the issues first, then enters into politics second. I would be quite happy to drop out of it.

"I would never sell my soul to get re-elected," she said. "I would never say what I don't believe.

"What I'd really like to do is make lots and lots of money and just be a writer of comedies, and sit at home with a lampshade on my head."

CHAPTER 9

POLITICAL BEGINNINGS

There tends to be a pattern in people's lives, which is why any sensible employer requires a curriculum vitae or work resume before hiring a new employee. That's what makes Campbell's stint as chairman of the Vancouver School Board so interesting. In her first term she was a novice and stayed in the background. In her second term she stepped on to centre stage, taking full advantage of her significant power. It could be seen as a dress rehearsal for the more important political positions she would assume later on. As will be seen, there is a distinct contrast between what she promised and what she delivered.

Campbell was one of 22 candidates who ran for the Vancouver School Board in the fall of 1982. There were nine positions on the board, and Carol Volkart of the *Sun* sent letters to each of them asking for personal details and what they'd do if elected. The resulting blurbs on each candidate were published on November 18, 1982. Campbell's reads as follows.

> *KIM CAMPBELL (NPA): A graduate of the University of B. C. and the London School of Economics, a political scientist, teacher and third-year law student, 35-year-old Kim Campbell is running for her second term on the school board. As a teacher at UBC and Langara, she said she's found her students display the results of great inconsistencies in school standards. Students should be protected from the luck of the draw and teachers should be accountable for what they do, she said.*
> *Campbell said trustees should set clear educational priorities instead of believing that all programs are of equal value. "We must have a clear sense of what we want to accomplish. There must be a clear commitment to the education of young minds."*

The statement is high-sounding but vague. Few would suspect from it that Campbell would focus her efforts on cutting school budgets as proved to be the case. Maybe the clue lies in the warning not to consider all programs of equal value. The implication may be that programs of lesser value should be dropped, but it's far from clear. The blurb also contains an interesting inaccuracy, namely that Campbell had graduated from the London School of Economics when she had not.

On voting day, November 18, Campbell topped the polls, winning more votes than any other NPA candidate, including Divinsky. She was elected chairman by a secret ballot of the NPA trustees. Less than two months later, Campbell launched upon a cost-cutting campaign which would dominate her entire term.

Rather than criticizing the government for imposing the cuts in education budgets, she criticized parents and teachers for resisting them.

She defended the provincial government's restraint program in a school board newsletter, noting that forestry, mining and corporate revenues were down. "I don't think any of the cuts will be a disaster," she insisted. "I simply see less room to manoeuvre and less room to take things for granted."

She stressed there would be no shortage of supplies such as paper. She acknowledged that innovative programs would be discouraged, commenting "that's a shame."

Things came to a head at a public meeting on January 10, 1983. Over a period of two hours, nine groups presented briefs. The associations representing 3,000 Vancouver teachers rejected salary cuts, layoffs, or changes in staffing levels. Parents argued for smaller class sizes, more help for immigrant children who couldn't speak English and a doubling of the number of schools that could accept handicapped children. The union representing support staff argued for increased staffing. Campbell's response was described in the *Sun* as a "tongue-lashing."

"This evening's presentations have been of marginal use to me as a trustee," Campbell said angrily. "It's unfortunate that those who are hands-on in the system, those with day-to-day expertise, that those people can't give us any guidelines about where cuts should be made."

She defended her approach in her interview with Volkart. "Let's not delude ourselves as to what was going on here," she said. "You have these little charades that take place and everybody is playing their role. That baffled me. It offends my sense of integrity."

Campbell said it didn't bother her if she was unpopular with the public. "Most people have an image of politicians as people who want to be loved. It's like being an entertainer. But I have discovered I don't need to be loved by the public; that I will only say what I think.

"I don't always say everything I think — that's part of being tactful — but I have been hissed and it doesn't bother me. As long as I'm saying what I really think, I'm prepared to stand by it."

At this time unemployed teachers were so numerous in Vancouver that the B.C. Teachers Federation set up a drop-in centre for them and got 25 to 30 drop-ins daily.

Opposition trustees accused Campbell and her NPA party of defending provincial Socred policies at the expense of the education system.

"She had no problem with restraint," says Phil Rankin. "She was totally anti-teacher. She'd always talk about her high regard for teachers and in her personal dealings with them it was awful, and shrill.

"She wasn't even particularly pro-administrator either. If anything went wrong, it was the people around her who had done something wrong, or they hadn't briefed her right. There was no way she'd take responsibility for any problem."

On May 16, Campbell cast the deciding ballot to pass the 1983 school board budget. The good news was that annual school taxes would drop $26 for the average Vancouver homeowner. The bad news was that school programs would be cut and teacher layoffs were likely in January.

A few months earlier Campbell had said she was not prepared to lay off staff. Now she said "drastic measures will have to be taken . . . and reductions in staff and services are inevitable."

Tempers were boiling, and in November the teachers went on strike. The school board promptly went to court for an injunction to prevent teachers from picketing schools. Campbell said she was worried the presence of picketers would cause serious confrontations. She maintained the strike was illegal. She told one reporter that she hoped the teachers would get "kicked in the ass."

In December, with school-board affairs in massive tumult, Campbell announced she would seek the Social Credit nomination to run in Vancouver centre in the next provincial election. Campbell was barely six months into a two-year term as school board chairman and already she was seeking other employment.

The Non-Partisan Association has always denied being a farm team for the Social Credit government, but Campbell's bid has every mark of a bid for the major league. Interviewed by Volkart on her reasons for running, Campbell said she thought it important that quality candidates stand for election. "Ultimately I have to believe that in a democracy people have to take responsibility for running."

So confident was she of winning, she already saw herself in cabinet. "I wouldn't mind being the next education minister for a while either, frankly," she said. "They need darn good women in that cabinet. People say, 'You wouldn't get a cabinet position in the first session anyway.' I say, 'Why not? They need me.'"

Campbell's plans were thwarted when she failed to win a seat in the Legislature. "She was abrasive and, of course, at that stage of her career it was easy to press that button and I did it at every opportunity," said Gary Lauk, the New Democrat who defeated her. "Every time she blew her cool at an all-candidates meeting I gained another 500 votes, which she realized afterwards."

Campbell's opponents on the Committee of Progressive Electors seized on her election bid under the Socred banner as proof of what they had suspected all along — the NPA was in cahoots with the Socreds. They issued a news release denouncing her. "We COPE school trustees will not silently watch the dismantling of public education while our chairperson sorts out the conflict between her political ambitions and her duty to speak for the needs of the Vancouver school district."

By this time Campbell had graduated from law school and was articling at a Vancouver law firm. She no longer needed the salary she got as school board chairman. Maybe her law firm wasn't thrilled to have one of its employees the centre of bitter controversy. On December 5, only half-way through her two-year term, Campbell resigned as chairman. She said she wanted to spend more time at her articling job. She also said she had felt "very, very pressured" over the previous few months.

"It's a very stressful time to be a trustee, period," she said. "It has been very, very difficult and the chairman bears the brunt of it.

"The nights that I'm not at the board, I'm at the firm. It doesn't leave much time for a personal life."

Campbell's school board career can be assessed from several angles. She had antagonized many parents and teachers and for them she was the villain of the piece, undermining the quality of the education system she had been elected to protect. But many property owners were no doubt pleased that she had managed to achieve a slight tax cut, and the Social Credit government of Bill Bennett must have been grateful to her for having taken so much flak implementing what was really a provincial initiative. Later Bennett would offer her a plum job in his office. Campbell had proven that she had an enormous capacity for work, holding down a full course load at law school while running the school board. Says Volkart: "She (Campbell) was efficient and organized and obviously very capable and smart but you didn't get a great feeling of warmth or humanity and you kind of wondered why she was doing this."

Campbell's life at this point was no triumphal procession. Her marriage had collapsed, she had quit her job as chairman of the school board amid controversy, she had been defeated in her bid for a seat in the legislature.

But her efforts had not gone unnoticed. She had caught the attention of some influential eyes. It's no fluke that Campbell was hired at Ladner Downs, one of the biggest and most prestigious law firms in Vancouver.

CHAPTER

10

THE BIG BLUE MACHINE

J.J. Camp is a tall, lean man with a gracious manner and impressive credentials in the legal community, having served as president of the Canadian Bar Association. He radiates decency and honesty, yet at the same time one suspects that he knows how to play hard ball if necessary. Camp plays a significant role in this saga for a couple of reasons, not least of which is that his firm gave Campbell her first job in the law business.

"I got to know her as a student and was one of those who recognized her as being potentially a very prominent lawyer," says Camp. "I urged the firm to keep her. We did offer her employment, she accepted that offer and stayed with us as a litigation lawyer for, I think a year and a half or something like that before she went back to politics." It's obvious that Camp was impressed by her.

"She was very, very competent," he continues. "Most of the time you see students who are much younger, who don't have the maturity, the street smarts, the worldliness that Kim has. She was poised to do very well. She was smart and worked hard and had all these additional attributes which served her very well."

Camp was struck by one Campbell trait in particular: "Kim and the word ambition went well together," he says. "She was always very ambitious from the time I met her. It was a remarkable feature of hers. And ambitious in a good sense. What I saw of her during the two and a half years I worked closely with her is consonant with what I've seen since. She's just a very ambitious person."

Camp says he hoped Campbell would stay with the firm but he knew that a law career was not her goal. "She was politically inclined from the moment I first met her," he says. "There was political blood coursing through her veins."

Camp is a distant relative of fabled Tory strategist Dalton Camp but plays down the connection, saying he has "never met the gentleman." He says that he is not part of Campbell's inner circle, although his colleague David Camp is. David Camp is Dalton's son.

These relationships are of more than passing interest in the Campbell story. Dalton Camp is the founder of what has become known as the Big Blue Machine, one of the most redoubtable organizations in modern Canadian politics, and it's a thesis of this book that Campbell owes her spectacular success in federal politics in good part to the backing of this political network.

There's nothing wrong with having an effective political organization, but Canadians are entitled to know how their political system works.

The term Big Blue Machine was coined by journalist Claire Hoy to describe the group of back-room political operatives who propelled Bill Davis to power as premier of Ontario time and again in the 1970s and early 1980s. The group introduced into Canada leading-edge media techniques which had been developed in the United States in particular by the Richard Nixon organization.

At the heart of the machine were two ex-Maritimers: Dalton Camp and his brother-in-law Norm Atkins. Camp made his reputation by unseating former Prime Minister John Diefenbaker and went on to found an advertising company called Camp Associates which would derive much of its business from serving Tory governments.

Camp and Atkins learned the art of getting and keeping power in New Brunswick, a province known for its fierce, clan-like and highly polarized politics. They still own next-door cottages at Robinson's Point, New Brunswick. Camp was a close friend of Richard Hatfield, the former Conservative premier of New Brunswick.

Over time Camp and Atkins gathered around them a pool of exceptional political talent — pollsters, speech-writers and bagmen. Camp Associates' official business was advertising, an art not far removed from the selling of political candidates. Its unofficial business was to provide a reservoir of top-notch political talent which could be drawn upon by Tories when needed.

Describing the Big Blue Machine in his biography of Bill Davis, Hoy notes its great success in raising money for political campaigns. That success was achieved in large part through old-fashioned Maritimes-style patronage where party donors were rewarded with government business in more or less direct proportion to their support.

Camp Associates itself thrived in large part thanks to tourism advertising contracted out by the Davis government, and there was a similar arrangement with the Hatfield government in New Brunswick. The machine was fueled by the governments which it kept in power. There was nothing terribly secret about the millions of dollars that Camp Associates earned advertising the scenic beauties of Ontario and New Brunswick and no one has claimed that money spent promoting tourism is wasted. However, as one veteran political reporter comments, "It was not too subtle."

Camp and Atkins both come across as kind and down-to-earth people and it is hard to believe they wield as much power as is attributed to them, but it's public knowledge that Atkins masterminded Mulroney's landslide victories of

1984 and 1988, and Camp's influence in the Progressive Conservative Party is said to be immeasurable.

Atkins makes no secret of his long-standing interest in Campbell. He says he first met her in 1982 and kept in touch with her after that first contact.

The meeting of Camp and Campbell may not quite rank with the pounding of the last spike but it was a significant moment nevertheless. The powerful current of the Big Blue Machine could now surge from Saint John to Vancouver.

The younger Camp is an intensely private person, and rarely talks to journalists. Judy Steed managed to get a few words with him when she was researching her Campbell profile. He told her about how he became friends with Campbell when they were both working at Ladner Downs and how he told his uncle, Norm Atkins, "You must meet this woman."

The three of them had dinner. "I was obviously impressed with her," says Atkins. "Because as a friend of David's, that would first of all impress me. But having said that, I was intrigued by her line of questioning in terms of what she was trying to gain from any conversation we might have about politics, about organization, about general things that would be of any political significance at that moment in time." Asked whether he already saw Campbell as potential new talent for the Conservative Party he says, "I don't think I could admit to that."

CHAPTER

11

THE BIG BLUE BACK ROOMS

In August 1985, Campbell received an offer to join the office of B.C. Premier Bill Bennett as executive director. She was recruited by Patrick Kinsella, a former Big Blue machinist from Ontario, who was Bennett's top aide. It was a plum job for someone who'd had no previous post with the Social Credit government.

"You will probably find me a little more reticent than before," she told reporters after Bennett announced her appointment. "I'm not going to shoot my mouth off like I did with the school board job." Campbell's job was to act as liaison between the premier's office and local riding associations. She was also supposed to prepare for the premier's public appearances, ensuring nothing untoward happened when Bennett ventured out of his office.

It didn't suit Campbell, to be continually preparing the way for someone else. As she said later, "In the premier's office you're working on communications strategy for people when you would rather be out there doing the communicating yourself."

While working in Bennett's office in Victoria, Campbell began dating Howard Eddy, a lawyer with the solicitor-general's ministry in Victoria. He's been described as tall and thin, a dead ringer for Abraham Lincoln. A mutual friend had told Campbell that Eddy was the most brilliant and creative person he knew. Campbell said that within a week of the time they started dating, they knew they would marry: "I'm a sucker for highly intelligent men." He was 10 years older than Campbell, had two adult sons and a teenage daughter. They lived aboard a 40-year-old, 14-metre cabin cruiser, Western Yew, moored in the marina at Sidney, B.C.

According to Campbell's sister, Alix, the relationship with Eddy was "crucial to Kim. she's not someone who likes to be alone, but she needs someone who can live with her demanding career."

Campbell later recalled the time fondly: "We would come aboard at the end of the day, take off our city clothes, and live in our own world."

On May 22, 1986, Bennett announced that he was resigning as premier, causing consternation in British Columbia. For Campbell, it meant her job was gone only six months after she'd started it, but this doesn't seem to have caused her much grief. She decided she would run for the premier's job.

From any rational perspective it was sheer folly. Campbell had barely joined the Social Credit Party, and already she was running to be its leader? She had never held a seat in the legislature and even her friends advised against it. David Camp had already committed to work for another candidate in the leadership race, Bud Smith. Camp met Campbell to talk her out of it and thought he had succeeded, but she stayed in the race, telling the media she had $50,000 to spend, and insisting she was in it to win.

As the leadership convention approached, the *Vancouver Sun* ran profiles on each of the 12 candidates. The piece on Campbell, written by Gillian Shaw, set a theme which has haunted her ever since.

> *Her conversation makes it clear she sees herself as a leader. Words like "enlighten" and "fostering growth" crop up when she talks about The People. "As an intellectually oriented person, I like to socialize with people who read the same things I do (Dostoevsky, Tolstoy, Jane Austen are authors she mentions) and have a similar level of education but I genuinely like ordinary people," she says. "I think it's very important to realize that a lot of people that you're out there working for are people who may sit in their undershirt and watch the game on Saturday, beer in hand." Campbell doesn't want to socialize with these people — "I suppose they would*

> *find me as boring as I would find them" — but she wants their votes so she can help them.*
>
> *"A lot of their attitudes you may not agree with, but they come from genuine human emotions — fear of change, fear of threat to their security," she says. "If you don't understand that and like people, you can't deal with them, you can't take them anywhere."*

Campbell has taken a lot of criticism for these remarks. They are said to reveal her as an elitist and a snob. But is it really a crime to prefer great literature to watching television? She does not criticize those who watch TV in their undershirts, merely stating that these are not her preferred pastimes.

Still, the issue is debatable. The phrase, "I genuinely like ordinary people," has the ring of someone who is protesting too much, it implies she does not consider herself to be ordinary. She is elevating herself above the common masses into some kind of aristocracy. Perhaps that is not surprising for a woman whose dominant early influences were Edmund Burke and Nathan Divinsky, both of whom defended the British class system. Ever since the Shaw article appeared she has been fighting the elitist image, especially by emphasizing her less glamorous summer jobs such as working in a fish packing plant or on the mayonnaise line at the Kraft factory. None of her official biographies provide details on how long she worked at these humble jobs and Rankin suggests it may have been only a few days.

Certainly by the time she entered her political career Campbell had distanced herself from that part of the population which must struggle to pay the rent. She told Gillian Shaw she had used the money she and Divinsky got out of their family home to put a down payment on a $210,000 house on Fairview Slopes. She said her five-per-cent non-voting shares in Jalm Holdings Ltd. were worth $60,000 to $100,000.

As part of her campaign for the Social Credit leadership, Campbell prepared a curriculum vitae loaded with personal information and containing a few puzzling details. This document indicates that Campbell won a Governor-General's award when attending St. Ann's Academy. This would have been unusual since the bronze medal is normally awarded to high school students and Campbell was in grade eight at the time. St. Ann's could find no record of the award. When questioned in May, 1993, a spokesperson for the office of the Governor-General also couldn't find such a record. However, in early September, when this book was at the printer, the same official provided a hand-written list of names including Campbell's.

The same curriculum vitae also states that Campbell had traveled internationally throughout Europe, Asia, the United States, Mexico and Caribbean countries. When did she do this traveling? Campbell had lived in London and had taken a three-month tour of the Soviet Union but is that equivalent to traveling "throughout"

Europe and Asia? And when did she travel to Mexico and the Caribbean? Possibly during her university years — but she has said she put herself through university skinning halibut at a Prince Rupert fish packing plant, working on the mayonnaise line at Kraft's Vancouver factory and working as a sleepwear clerk at the Bay.

CHAPTER

12

TROUNCED

Campbell staged her entrance at the Social Credit leadership convention with a kilted piper playing "The Campbells are Coming." Each of the 12 candidates delivered a speech before the final vote and she drew the second-last spot. It was a stroke of luck because she got to deliver her speech on prime time, when the television audience was the biggest. She used the free publicity for a veiled attack on the front-runner, Vander Zalm. "To be credible a leader must show an ability to grasp and understand these complex issues," she said. "In this day and age a leader cannot deceive the public with a simplistic vision of the past that cannot be recaptured. Even the slickest salesmanship cannot sell for long on a vision that is essentially empty, a vision that is really only a memory. It is fashionable to speak of leaders in terms of their charisma. Charisma without substance is a dangerous thing. It raises expectations which cannot be fulfilled and leads to disillusionment in a leader."

The line about a "simplistic vision of the past that cannot be recaptured" was a veiled reference to Vander Zalm's Christian world view with its emphasis on traditional family values. The punch line about charisma without substance brought cheers from a good part of the crowd — the anti-Vander Zalm faction — and is quoted frequently to this day, sometimes directed against Campbell herself. She did not name her target but the crowd knew exactly who she was talking about, including Vander Zalm.

"At the time I was doing so well it didn't bother me a whole lot," he says.

For Vander Zalm's numerous critics, Campbell's speech was a highlight of the evening. B.C. journalist Stan Persky called it "hands down, the most thoughtful speech of the night. Although Campbell could barely find enough people in the hall to hold her campaign banner aloft, she offered the closest thing to an alternative vision for Social Credit." Jim Hume of the *Victoria Times-Colonist* called Campbell "the star of the show."

Not everyone was so impressed. Denny Boyd of the *Vancouver Sun*, said Campbell "appeared to be delivering a reform lecture rather than a campaign speech, broken only by a few inside jokes. Heavy on policy, low on personality." Geoffrey Stevens of the *Globe and Mail* described her campaign as "pathetic." The most enthusiastic review came from Campbell herself years later. "A lot of people thought I gave the campaign some kind of legitimacy," she told Peter Newman. "There were two winners at that convention. One was Bill Vander Zalm and the other was me." Campbell has always demonstrated an ability, probably essential in a politician, to interpret all her setbacks as successes, but she was not a big winner at the convention by conventional standards. She was automatically eliminated in the first ballot.

Vander Zalm won with a healthy margin despite Campbell's attack and Campbell finished 12th in a field of 12, collecting just 14 out of 1,294 votes cast.

David Camp's preferred candidate was also defeated so he and Campbell had something to console each other about afterwards. According to Heather Bird, Camp admired Campbell for running even though she had done so against his advice.

> *Camp looks back on that experience and realizes she was right to run but wrong to go about it the way she did. "She was absolutely right in that she knew she had something to say and others weren't saying it," he says. But he did take her out again. This time to press home the point that in politics, you need a team to succeed. In an achingly poignant reference to her unhappy adolescence, Camp says she looked across the table and said:*

> *"David, you've got to understand. It's very hard for me to ask for help. It's something that I have to overcome." Camp says, "She really felt left to her own resources (as a teenager) . . . I felt bad for her that she wouldn't ask people to help her."*

He recognized her plea for help and was ready to offer that help. Indeed, their friendship seems to have developed into something far deeper than the usual marriages of convenience that characterize the political world. As Campbell's campaign manager during her successful bid for the Tory leadership, he claimed in all seriousness to be doing the job with no personal agenda in mind. "This is a once-in-a-lifetime thing," he told Judy Steed. "It'll never happen to me again. I'm dedicated to her. It's very important to her to know she's got people around her who don't have a personal agenda, who aren't clinging to her for their own personal reasons."

Like Campbell, Camp has political blood in his veins, but he is not inclined to take a public role. Campbell on the other hand is a born candidate, who loves being in the public eye, but until she met Camp she lacked the back room organization that is vital in today's political arena. It seems clear that Campbell from this time became increasingly a part of the eastern-rooted Tory network which had been founded by Dalton Camp and Norm Atkins. Whether it's called the Big Blue Machine or something else is unimportant; it is a powerful network and when she connected with it, her political fortunes improved dramatically. Four months after the 1986 Social Credit leadership convention, Vander Zalm called an election and Campbell ran victoriously in Vancouver-Point Grey.

It's not clear how she managed to fund the effort so soon after spending some $40,000 to $50,000 in her failed bid for the Socred leadership. Political campaigns don't come cheap. Campbell's main assets were her residence and her shares in Jalm Holdings, which she did not sell until 1989. She must have had some good fund-raisers.

When the victorious Vander Zalm named his cabinet, Campbell was not on the list.

She made no secret of her irritation at having been left out. It was widely assumed that the premier held a grudge for the "charisma without substance" remark at the convention although he denies it. "You can't put everybody in the cabinet" he says. "Some get included, some get left out. You have to balance it off and she had no experience."

CHAPTER

13

DUMPING VANDER ZALM

One of Campbell's lesser-known accomplishments is her contribution to the demise of Bill Vander Zalm's political career.

Even though Campbell and Vander Zalm shared some common beliefs about free-enterprise capitalism, they were as unlike as fire and water. Campbell was a worldly-wise skeptic, an intellectual, a self-proclaimed pro-choice feminist. He was almost childlike in his simplicity, a self-educated man whose bookshelf carried more books about gardening than about political science. He seemed blissfully unaware of the unwritten axiom of Canadian political life that religion and politics don't mix. As he put it, "I want to bring to government high moral standards based on true Christian principles."

During Bill Bennett's day, the Social Credit government had been relatively in-synch with the federal Tory machine. Eastern Conservatives like David Camp and Patrick Kinsella could readily work with the Socreds, and did. Vander Zalm was another story. He owed nothing to the Big Blue Machine, its descendants or accessories, and its operatives had no influence over him.

Vander Zalm also had problems with the media who portrayed him as a lunatic and a crook, even though he was probably no crazier or crookeder than a number of other politicians. Richard Hatfield ran a highly organized kick-back system in New Brunswick for years and his personal habits were far stranger than Vander Zalm's. Hatfield used to throw wild parties for members of the legislature press gallery, daring reporters to strip naked and run through the lobby of the Fredericton's Lord Beaverbrook Hotel, or to go skinny-dipping in his neighbor's swimming pool. For some reason it was understood that Hatfield's antics could not be reported and he was portrayed for many years as a progressive and dignified statesman while Vander Zalm was portrayed as an utter fool.

It stands to reason that political networks seek to extend their influence, and to eliminate those who play by idiosyncratic rules. When Vander Zalm won the Social Credit leadership he called it a victory of "the shovel over the machine." The shovel for him was a symbol of his humble, grass-roots beginnings. But the machine had not been put out of commission, far from it. It would wreak its vengeance on him, and Campbell would play a significant role in the process.

The opportunity came on January 28, 1988, when the Supreme Court of Canada struck down Canada's abortion law. The law had required that abortions be permitted only after a committee of at least three doctors issued a written certificate saying continuation of the pregnancy would endanger a woman's "life or health."

The court struck down the law on the grounds that it violated a woman's right to "life, liberty and security of the person."

Vander Zalm opposed abortion on religious grounds and announced that, despite the Supreme Court decision, British Columbia's Medicare plan would not fund abortions. This caused an uproar that dominated B.C. politics for weeks and spilled over to become a major national story.

Kim Campbell and J.J. Camp moved against Vander Zalm in a highly effective one-two operation. Campbell moved first by publicly denouncing the premier's abortion policy. As Greg Weston puts it, "Campbell stepped up to the microphone and blasted her own premier with a force that launched her into the national limelight."

According to Mark Kennedy of the *Citizen*, "Campbell became the first member of caucus to speak out and within a day she became a national news story." Campbell was eventually joined by four other MLAs who could not accept Vander Zalm's policy.

While Campbell challenged the premier's abortion policy in the media, J.J. Camp challenged the policy in court. He filed a petition on behalf of the B.C. Civil Liberties Association, saying the cabinet "had failed to take into account highly relevant considerations" when it drafted its regulations.

On March 7, B.C. Supreme Court Justice Allan McEachern struck down the provincial abortion policy. Vander Zalm acknowledges that the defeat was a major blow to his credibility.

"The abortion issue was the turning point for Bill Vander Zalm," says the former premier. "Things were actually going quite well up until the abortion issue flared up, and then many within the media turned against me."

CHAPTER 14

KIM GOES FEDERAL

If it's true that Kim Campbell wanted to be prime minister from early childhood, as some claim, it's surprising she didn't run for a seat in the Commons until she was forty-one. Campbell herself denies such a childhood ambition, saying she really wanted to be secretary-general of the United Nations. Celebrities don't always control the mythology that churns up in their wake.

Those who search for a systematic plan in Campbell's life, search in vain. "People have written that somehow I calculated a step-by-step approach to what I'm doing now," she says. "If you look at my career, you see it wasn't like that." Once, when an interviewer asked if she would run for the Conservative leadership should Mulroney resign, she replied, "Life is unpredictable. I might run for the leadership or I might run away with a gigolo to Brazil."

Campbell has said it was the free trade issue that brought her into federal politics. Even though she had never before shown much interest in economic matters, she apparently felt so strongly about the Canada-U.S. Free Trade Agreement that she could not bear to sit on the sidelines during the 1988 election in which it was the major issue. She told Tim Harper of the *Toronto Star* the decisive moment came when she heard Liberal Leader John Turner deliver one of his speeches denouncing the deal. "It showed me the type of campaign this was going to be," she said. "I couldn't believe what I was hearing. It curled my hair."

But there's another line which is not consistent with the first. She told Steve Mertl of *The Canadian Press* she might not have run federally if Vander Zalm had given her a place in his cabinet. "I didn't get the opportunity to do a lot of things that I wanted to get done (at the provincial level)," she said. "That wasn't my choice. For some reason the premier didn't want to put me in cabinet. A lot of my colleagues wanted to see me there."

Senator Atkins, the Conservatives' national campaign manager in the election of 1988, says he tried to persuade Campbell to run against Turner but she refused because she didn't think she could beat Turner. "Also, she was a member of the provincial legislature and she didn't want to move from something and resign from something into something that didn't have some potential," he says.

Campbell gave yet another version of her motives to Commons Speaker John Fraser, who is a staunch environmentalist, telling him her mission was "saving the planet." Like Mulroney, Campbell has a chameleon-like way of adapting the message to the audience.

On September 22, 1988, just five days before Mulroney called the election of that year, Tory veteran Pat Carney announced her retirement as MP for Vancouver Centre. It was by no means a Tory fortress, but it was an incumbent riding which Carney had held for two terms.

Carney said she was retiring for health reasons — she had arthritis. However, her arthritis did not prevent her from accepting an appointment to the Senate a short time later. Coincidentally, Carney and Campbell are related through marriage. Carney's cousin Marguerite Parkinson is George Campbell's third wife. Despite this connection, the Carney-Campbell relationship is rumored to be cool at best.

Vancouver Centre is one of the more volatile ridings in Canada. It takes in Vancouver's downtown core and Stanley Park, and reportedly has the highest concentration of gays and lesbians in Canada.

Some Vancouver voters criticized Campbell for quitting her seat in the provincial Legislature in mid-term, an unusual move which would trigger a provincial by-election at public expense. *Maclean's* quoted Lee Durkin, a waiter who lived and worked in the riding, as saying he wouldn't vote for her: "She jumped too quickly from provincial to federal politics, from party to party. That was opportunistic."

Campbell's main opponent in the race was national NDP president, Johanna den Hertog, then considered a potential NDP leader. The most memorable moment in the campaign occurred when Campbell lost her temper at an all-candidates meeting, shouting at anti-free-trade hecklers: "What are you afraid of? What are you afraid of?" The cameras were rolling and the clip got extensively play on television screens across the country.

Campbell won the riding by a tight 269-vote margin, bucking the trend that gave the NDP 19 of 32 seats in the province. "We knew every vote counted," said Campbell. "Anyone who was thought to be a Tory was dragged to the polls." Vancouver Centre was reportedly one of two seats that Mulroney watched most closely on that election night.

Even though Campbell and Mulroney hadn't met, he had no doubt been briefed about the new up-and-comer. When Campbell was named Justice Minister some 15 months later, *Maclean's* noted that her rapid rise had been predicted by many senior Tories:

> *In a government eagerly in search of promising new faces to groom for its beleaguered front bench, many Tories had noted Campbell's willingness to vigorously and eloquently defend controversial Tory policies such as the Meech Lake constitutional accord and the impending Goods and Services Tax.*

Said William Fox, an Ottawa consultant and former Mulroney communications adviser, "Kim has been followed closely from the time she was a candidate. She is tough, intelligent and very much a team player."

Campbell professed to be lukewarm about the move to Ottawa, even though it opened up a whole array of new career possibilities. "People who think that's my single ambition don't realize what the negatives are," she told Peter Newman. "Brian Mulroney is from Montreal, his friends and family are all within easy commuting distance. If he wants to have a gang up at Harrington Lake for the weekend, his friends can go. My family and friends are on the West coast, so those opportunities are not there."

She left her stylish three-story house in Vancouver to take over Carney's 1,000-square-foot, two-bedroom apartment in Ottawa and noted with some annoyance that the rent on the apartment, $1,200 a month, was higher than her house maintenance costs in Vancouver. Her husband Howard Eddy quit his job with the B.C. government to join her in Ottawa. True to form, Campbell had barely unpacked her Inuit carvings before she was publicly speculating about her cabinet prospects.

"I would be surprised if I wasn't in consideration but it's a matter for the Prime Minister to decide," she told Steve Mertl. She was in fact attractive cabinet material, not least because she was a woman. Atkins is explicit on this point: "It was part of the Mulroney mandate to find women who had the capacity to take on major responsibilities and to give them those responsibilities. I think she stood out as one of those."

When the House of Commons opened its new session, Campbell was given the honor of seconding the speech from the throne. Mulroney stayed in the House to listen to her speech, another honor not usually accorded backbenchers. When she delivered part of the speech in French, he swiveled in his seat, apparently astonished at her fluency in French.

Campbell admitted to Newman later she had got some of the speech translated and it was really a matter of reading it. "I was surprised and pleased that people were so impressed. I'm sure the Prime Minister was interested in it but I don't think, in and of itself, that was enough to get me in cabinet. The fact that I was chosen to give the address in reply to the Speech from the Throne suggests he wanted to make some gesture towards me. But that was early December 1988 and it wasn't until the end of January 1989 that he made the first big cabinet change and I was appointed."

From early December to late January is only two months. It might have seemed a long time to Campbell but if one considers the pace of most MPs' careers, it looks more like the fast track.

The signal that she was to be promoted came with a phone call one Friday afternoon from Stanley Hartt, then the Prime Minister's chief of staff, summoning her to Ottawa. When she arrived in Ottawa, Hartt called her again and told her the Prime Minister wanted to see her at 7:45. She assumed he meant 7:45 the next morning, and went out for dinner with her husband. It turned out that Hartt had meant 7:45 that evening. It was a novice politician's nightmare; after having flown across the country at the prime minister's behest, she had missed the rendez-vous by getting the time confused.

Fortunately for Campbell, Mulroney was understanding. "In the end he did call me and was unbelievably sweet and asked me to join the cabinet as minister of state for Indian affairs and northern development. All I remember saying is, 'Oh thank you, thank you, thank you.'"

As junior minister of Indian affairs, Campbell was essentially an understudy for the senior minister, Tom Siddon. Junior ministers fill in when the senior minister is out of town or can't make it to an engagement of secondary importance. Robert Fife says that "her relatively few responsibilities entitled her to a driver and a limousine, a staff of 12 and an array of offices. Campbell's salary and tax-free allowances amounted to more than $130,000 annually, including a $2,000 car subsidy, a leftover from bygone decades when ministers were not provided with chauffeur-driven limousines."

Despite considerable tumult in native affairs across Canada, Campbell avoided controversy, made few noteworthy pronouncements and remained little-known to the general public. A search for press clippings about Campbell during this period turns up little.

It wasn't until February 1990, when Mulroney named her the first female justice minister, that Campbell began getting significant notice from the national media.

Justice is one of the most prestigious portfolios in the federal cabinet. Louis St. Laurent, John Turner, Jean Chretien and Pierre Trudeau all served in justice before going on to their party's leadership. In elevating Campbell to this lofty post when she had less than two years' experience, Mulroney had given her a tremendous boost. Peter Newman gives an entertaining account of how she learned the news:

> *She had just arrived home in Vancouver to help explain the new budget. She got another call from Stanley Hartt telling her that the prime minister wanted all his ministers in their seats for the budget presentation. She promptly went into her western-alienation rant: "No wonder we never get elected, nobody cares if I'm in my seat in the House, somebody else can take my place in the House, somebody else can take my place, it's important for me to be here to explain the budget to people on the ground, blah, blah."*
> *Hartt didn't bat an eye, saying only, "Well the prime minister would like all the ministers in their seat on Tuesday*

and he would like to have a chat with you Thursday afternoon." Campbell wasn't giving up that easily. Later she told Hartt she would take the 6:30 flight out on Thursday because she was scheduled to speak to the Victoria Chamber of Commerce on the Meech Lake accord. "You will not be able to make your speaking engagement," Hartt replied, his nerves at high-wire tension, "and what's more, you'll be so happy, blocks will melt in your mouth."

"So I went out, and my staff couldn't realize why I wasn't more pissed off about being called back," she recalls. "I was fairly chipper. 'Oh dear, well, that's the way it is. I guess the prime minister wants us there in our seats. Oh well, solidarity, you know, and all that.'" She received a message on Thursday afternoon that the prime minister wanted to see her at 24 Sussex at 5:15, and she actually got there on time. At 5:40, Mulroney rushed in to say they'd have to talk in the car because there was a vote in the House at 6 o'clock. "So we put our coats and boots on and jump into the back of his car, and he has a motorcade. We're whizzing through the streets of Ottawa with the lights flashing and he's saying. . . cabinet shuffle tomorrow, blah, blah . . . you'll be sworn in as the minister of justice,

attorney-general of Canada. My chief of staff is waiting for me in the lobby and I kind of smile at him, and we go in and do the vote. I come out, and my office is in the West Block, which is linked to the Centre Block by a tunnel, so Michael Ferrabee and I walk down the stairs and get into the elevator. We're the only ones on it. As soon as the door closes, I yell out that I'm going to be sworn in as the new minister of justice and attorney general of Canada. We were hugging each other and jumping up and down until the elevator stopped. Then we just walked out calmly, not daring to look at one another."

Is it not unusual for a cabinet minister to embrace her chief of staff in an elevator? If the cabinet minister had been a male and the chief of staff a female, would such conduct be considered acceptable? Campbell speaks so freely in the interview with Newman one has the impression that she either did not know she was being recorded or did not think Newman would use her comments so freely.

Most cabinet ministers avoid using expressions such as "pissed off" in interviews when they know they may be quoted. They may use such common expressions in private but generally stick to more dignified vocabulary in public and interviews.

Perhaps she felt so comfortable with Newman that she trusted him to do the editing.

If so she erred, for his story caused her serious problems during the Conservative leadership race.

The kicker in this anecdote is that Mulroney gives a completely different version of what happened. According to Robert Fife, Mulroney says that he and Campbell were in the prime minister's study when he informed her of his plans to name her justice minister.

It seems odd that the two parties would be at variance over such a simple point. If Mulroney told Campbell she would be justice minister while they were speeding along in a motorcade with flashing lights, it must have been a memorable experience. It is unlikely that either of them would forget it quickly. Yet Mulroney says he gave her the news in his study and she says he told her in a speeding car. It's only a trifle, but the Campbell story is strewn with such trifles.

CHAPTER

15

TOWARDS A JUSTICE PORTFOLIO

Campbell entered the justice portfolio full of bravado, confidently brushing aside questions about her lack of experience. "It has taken me ten years to become an overnight sensation," she proclaimed. She said her overarching goal was "to have a system of justice and laws that reflects women's reality." Elaborating on this theme in an interview with David Vienneau of the *Toronto Star,* she said Canadian laws work against women because they were written by men, and men can't get pregnant.

"I reached puberty at the age of eleven," she told Vienneau. "Now, I wasn't sexually active at the time, but the point is that for much of my life now, the question of controlling my fertility has been a major preoccupation . . . Men just don't face that and the reality of what it means."

Skeptics might wonder what relevance the experience of pregnancy has to most laws, but in any case it's surprising that Campbell would say controlling her fertility was a major preoccupation, since she had known for many years she was infertile. Fife confirmed this with her mother Lissa Vroom and with a family friend:

> *Lissa says that her daughter was told by doctors she 'could not conceive.' A friend of the family said there was 'great sadness' in the household at that time and that Campbell became 'rather listless' when she was not able to have a child.*

When she talks about the anti-female bias of the justice system, she may be thinking of how women have traditionally been penalized for unwanted pregnancies while men have escaped with no penalties.

"If you look at human history, men complain occasionally that they were 'shot-gunned' into marriage," she told Vienneau. "But it is women who have been dishonored and driven to the streets and driven to desperation over the years from unwanted pregnancy or simply through surrendering to their passions in socially inappropriate contexts."

The words Campbell uses are emotionally charged, and it's clear that abortion is an issue on which she feels strongly. She had made her passionate pro-choice position clear at the time of her break with Vander Zalm. It's scarcely surprising that, before her brief term as justice minister was over, the government had accepted unrestricted access to abortion as the de facto law of the land in Canada.

The abortion issue had been hanging over the government ever since January, 1988, when the Supreme Court of Canada struck down the federal abortion law. Many feminists were pleased that the law had been struck down and did not want the government to replace it. Campbell made no secret of her feelings on the issue. "I am among those Canadians who are very comfortable without a law," she said in the Commons shortly before she was named to the justice portfolio.

It's strange that Mulroney would appoint a strong pro-choicer such as Campbell to the justice portfolio at a time when the government was trying to pass legislation which contradicted the pro-choice position. This is rather like appointing a passionate vegetarian to manage a hamburger stand. Some observers felt the legislation was designed to fail from the beginning. According to this scenario, Mulroney's inner circle privately favored the politically correct option of abortion on demand but realized this policy could not be introduced openly without substantial political cost. Even though pro-choicers overwhelmingly dominated debate in the media, public opinion polls showed that the majority of Canadians wanted some restrictions on access to abortion.

A Gallup Poll done in October 1992 indicated that only 31 per cent of Canadians believed abortion should be legal under any circumstances, while 67 percent favored restrictions of varying degrees. Clearly, most Canadians wanted some kind of law.

The restrictions in the government's proposed legislation were minimal. Basically, abortion would be legal if one physician determined that carrying the baby to term would endanger the mother's physical or mental health. Explanatory notes accompanying the bill defined "health" very broadly. In effect, any woman who wanted an abortion would simply have to find a single doctor who was willing to say that her psychological or emotional well-being might be at risk if the baby was carried to term. The old law had required approval by a committee.

Even though the law provided broad access to abortion, it did give doctors the option of saying no, and did provide criminal penalties for abortions performed without a physician's inquiry into the circumstances of the case. Pro-choice groups were furious with Campbell for supporting the new legislation and accused her of betraying her principles. She was in an awkward position but managed to sound fairly eloquent in defending the bill.

> *Just as I am deeply opposed to the notion of a woman not being able to obtain an abortion when she wants it, I think it is equally tragic for a woman to have an abortion which she later regrets. Now that is part of human life*

> *and we all do things which we may later regret, but I think it is extremely important that when a woman goes to a doctor with a request for something as serious as a termination of a pregnancy that there at least be an inquiry as to whether that decision is an informed decision, whether it is based on a realistic evaluation of the circumstance.*

Pro-life groups were unhappy with the bill because it would allow virtually free access to abortion, but some of them accepted it as better than nothing. Bill Janzen of the Mennonite Central Committee, who followed the debate closely, was impressed by Campbell's performance. "She urged people to recognize that in a society where there were some very deeply held convictions, some compromise should be made by all sides and in that sense she got some credit from pro-life people. They described her as being a team player."

The bill passed the Commons but was defeated in the Senate by a tie vote of 43-43. It was Senator Pat Carney who flew in from Vancouver to cast the crucial vote.

Under the Canadian constitution, the Senate has the power to block legislation, but it is scarcely ever used. The last time the Senate vetoed a bill was in the 1930s. If the government was committed to a law on abortion, as it claimed to be, it could have found a way to push it through. The government did not allow the

Senate to thwart its will on legislation to which it really was committed, such as the bill implementing the free-trade deal. But Justice Minister Campbell accepted the tie-vote on abortion as an adequate excuse for dropping the legislation. "Democracy has spoken," she said, even though the final outcome had been determined by a chamber of non-elected politicians.

Feminists were generally pleased with the outcome of the abortion battle, but they were not pleased with Campbell's performance on gun control. Women had lobbied tirelessly for a total ban on semi-automatic weapons such as the Sturm Ruger used by Marc Lepine in the appalling Montreal Polytechnique massacre. Her gun-control legislation left weapons such as the Sturm Ruger available for purchase by anyone who could get two references and pay a $50 fee. Almost anyone who wanted one could obtain these weapons. Feminists saw this as an unexpected and shocking sell-out to the gun lobby given the media attention and public revulsion that had focused on the accessibility of these deadly weapons and the crimes committed with them.

Despite the major issues she dealt with in the justice portfolio, Campbell remained much less known than other cabinet ministers such as Michael Wilson and Joe Clark. What finally gave her true national prominence was nothing that she said or did, but a picture by freelance portrait photographer Barbara Woodley in which Campbell is holding a black lawyer's robe on a hanger in front of her.

The picture had been taken some two years earlier but attracted little notice until it was splashed across the front page of the *Ottawa Citizen*, whereupon it became the centre of a national controversy. New Democrat MP Lynn Hunter said she didn't think MPs should use their sexuality to draw attention to themselves and called Campbell "the Madonna of Canadian politics," but Tory MP Barbara Greene said the picture revealed Campbell's tremendous sense of humor: "She is an absolutely hilarious woman."

There are conflicting versions of how the picture was taken. According to photographer Woodley, Campbell had no hesitation about removing her blouse for the picture, and "immediately complied" when Woodley asked her to do so. But Campbell later claimed she was fully clothed when the picture was taken.

The natural inference for anyone seeing Campbell's bare shoulders in the photograph is that Campbell is standing naked behind the robe, and the news value of the picture is precisely in that suggestion. Probably no cabinet minister in the entire Commonwealth had ever before posed for a photograph hinting at nudity.

Although opposition critics professed to be scandalized, the picture did wonders for Campbell's public recognition. Senator Atkins believes it was a significant factor in her rapid rise to power. The photo generated three waves of publicity — the first after it was run in the *Citizen*, the second when it was picked up by newspapers in Britain and the third when it was picked up in Japan.

Although Campbell was experiencing great success in her public life, she took another big blow in her private life with the abrupt departure of her second husband. She was apparently taken by surprise, arriving home after work one day to find his clothing gone. She admitted her devastation in a speech to a group of women journalists: "In the course of my life in Ottawa my marriage has ended and I'm very far from home. I find the life here often unspeakably lonely and very difficult."

CHAPTER

16

GAY AND LESBIAN RIGHTS

When U.S. President Bill Clinton tried to lift the ban on gays and lesbians in the military there was a national uproar which dominated the news for weeks and he was eventually forced to backtrack. In Canada, the same thing was accomplished with scarcely any controversy due to a little-noted decision by Kim Campbell during her term as justice minister. In effect, she brought about an important shift in policy on gay and lesbian rights without introducing legislation or even issuing a press release. The story was missed by the mainstream press and it's suspected that even some of Campbell's own cabinet colleagues did not realize her role in what had happened.

The Tories have not traditionally been a party to welcome liberal sexual values but Mulroney has a special interest in gay rights because his younger brother is gay. That may account for the Tory commitment in 1985 to ban discrimination against gays and lesbians in areas under federal jurisdiction.

On December 10, 1992, Campbell attempted to follow through on that promise with amendments to the Canadian Human Rights Act. Under her proposal, sexual orientation would become a prohibited grounds for discrimination. However, a group of Tory MPs known as the family caucus vigorously resisted the bill saying they did not want to fight the next election as the party which had enshrined gay and lesbian rights.

After much internal wrangling the bill was allowed to slide onto the back burner. It appeared that the family caucus had won the day, but Campbell would achieve her objectives by another route.

She did so by taking advantage of a court challenge to the Canadian Human Rights Act which had been launched in December, 1990 by Ottawa gay-rights activist Graham Haig and former air force captain Joshuah Birch.

The suit charged that Birch's opportunities for advancement in the air force had been blocked because he was gay. The policy in the forces at this time was that gays and lesbians could serve but would not be promoted. In August 1992, the Ontario Court of Appeal accepted the Haig-Birch complaint as valid. Using a controversial "reading in" technique to reach its decision, the court said the Canadian Human Rights Act should be read as if it covered sexual orientation as a prohibited grounds for discrimination. In effect, the court amended the act.

The novelty of this approach should be underlined. Under the Canadian constitution, it is for Parliament to make laws while the courts are supposed to interpret the laws. But in the Haig-Birch case the court went beyond what has been traditionally understood as interpretation to add a significant new element to the legislation.

The far-reaching importance of the Haig-Birch ruling was not fully appreciated by the public or the mainstream press, but it was hailed with delight in the gay community.

"The Haig Birch decision is a major victory for lesbian and gay rights," commented the Toronto-based gay newspaper *XTRA!* "For the first time, any discrimination in areas of federal jurisdiction can be brought before a human rights tribunal."

Campbell could have appealed the Haig-Birch ruling but she chose not to do so. Through this simple decision she was able to accomplish virtually the same objective that had been denied her by the family caucus. And if there was any doubt about the matter, it was eliminated by another ruling that came hard on the heels of Haig-Birch.

Michelle Douglas, a former second lieutenant in the Canadian Armed Forces, had launched a lawsuit in 1992 claiming she had been driven out the forces because she was lesbian. Once again Campbell could have fought the judgment but chose not to do so. On August 27, 1992, Justice Department lawyers announced in Federal Court that the case would be settled through something known as a consent order. The government paid Douglas $100,000 as compensation for the discrimination she had suffered plus court costs.

The effect of this settlement was to lift restrictions on gays and lesbians in the military, and in private meetings with gay and lesbian activists, Campbell took full credit for this historic policy change. Doug Sanders, a UBC law professor, was one of a group of activists who discussed the Douglas case with Campbell in the fall of 1992.

"She made a point of saying to us that she had settled the Douglas case," says Sanders. "That is what she described as having happened. She made the decision that Department of Justice lawyers would not fight the case. They would show up in court and agree to a consent order which ended the ban on lesbians and gays (in the military).

"She spoke with pride: 'We've done it three months before the United States.' Because at that point it was expected that Clinton would pull it off as soon as he came in (to office).

"I think one of the aspects of it very clearly was, it was perceived as, 'the courts made us do it.' whereas if you look at what happened and her description of it is accurate, the courts didn't make them do it, the Department of Justice made a decision which she takes credit for."

Sanders believes that Campbell deliberately played down her role in the decision so as to avoid a battle with the family caucus, and he argues convincingly that the strategy worked. Shortly after the Douglas case, family caucus member Donald Blenkarn was quoted as accepting the new policy with resignation: "We can't keep fighting court cases."

Sanders notes that "he (Blenkarn) went along with it seeing it as something the courts had foisted on the government. It was manipulated a little bit."

Once again, the general public did not fully understand what was being accomplished in these complicated court maneuvers, but the gay and lesbian community was better informed. Campbell discussed the changes in a November 17 interview with writers for *XTRA!*. "Over the summer the legal environment has changed quite dramatically with respect to the issue of sexual orientation," she said. "It was our decision not to appeal Haig. The result of that is basically to change the human rights act and to provide sexual orientation as a prohibited grounds of discrimination in the act which means that anyone who wishes to lodge a complaint in this area can do that."

The interviewer for *XTRA!* pressed Campbell on whether she was still committed to adding the words "sexual orientation" as a prohibited grounds for discrimination under the Canadian Human Rights Act. She replied, "For all intents and purposes it is in the law now."

It might be expected that Campbell's efforts would make her popular with the gay and lesbian constituency, but this is not necessarily the case.

"I don't think the Tories have done anything for us," says Chris Phibbs, a Toronto lesbian. "She (Campbell) could have included those amendments in the human rights act but she didn't do it.

"The government is supposed to be leading and the courts are supposed to be following but she is allowing the courts to determine public policy. Instead of bringing in legislation they say, 'The courts are forcing us to do this.' They don't want to go to the polls the next time as the government that gave equal rights to gays and lesbians because they think that would bring them down in flames. Why should the (gay and lesbian) community have to fight all these court battles one at a time? First it's rights in the military then it's rights for adoption, then it's pensions. This is not a cheap thing to do and it's time consuming. Why don't they come right out and say it — gays and lesbians have equal rights?"

Those who uphold full rights for gays and lesbians and those who have reservations about the gay lifestyle would probably agree with Phibbs on this point: If Campbell wants to advance the cause of gay rights she should do so openly by bringing in legislation rather than allowing the courts to "write in" laws that the politicians don't have the courage to write themselves.

CHAPTER

17

HEADSTART

The government of Brian Mulroney faced an extremely difficult situation in its second term. The election of 1988 had been as hard-fought, probably, as any in Canadian history and the Conservatives won in large part by convincing Canadians that the free trade deal would ensure their economic security. When the deal was followed not by prosperity but by widespread plant closures and massive job losses, a significant portion of the electorate felt betrayed. Blaming an international recession did not improve the public mood.

Mulroney professed to be unbothered as his standing in the polls dropped from one record low to another but his sagging face and puffy eyes told another story. Within his own party, behind the public display of solidarity, the troops were getting restless.

As Dalton Camp puts it, "There was a kind of universal wish in the party that something happen, that there be new leadership before the next election, and no one was willing or able or wanting to do anything about it in any overt way but nevertheless sort of a wish list developing."

One of the key questions for anyone trying to understand Campbellmania is how Campbell came to be designated as a front runner in the leadership race before it had even begun. Camp describes the process as informal and spontaneous, definitely not the result of any particular group imposing its agenda on the party.

"Nobody sat down and said, 'We're going to promote this person as the next Prime Minister of Canada,' not to my knowledge.

"One of the things that happens all the time when people say, 'You know, the leader's unpopular, the leader's got to go' is people say, 'Well what would we do without him, who have you got in mind? There isn't anybody.'

"And then there's this consensus growing about certain people and of course the wish list in the party involves Campbell, and I guess at the end of it all, she was the only one who was left standing, all the rest of them dropped out."

Camp says he was delighted when Campbell won the leadership. "I wanted a prime minister who didn't come from Quebec or from Central Canada, someone who came from somewhere else and ideally British Columbia. In the second place, I wanted a woman as prime minister if we possibly could find one. And I thought she met both of those criteria admirably.

"My son (David Camp) early on started sending me copies of her speeches and I recall writing a column something like two or three years ago that she was making the best speeches of anybody in the cabinet on the issues of the economy and the GST and constitution."

Camp denies that the Big Blue Machine entered its second generation when his son David became Campbell's friend, adviser and ultimately campaign manager.

"I think he (David) is his own piece of work. I would have considered him kind of a free agent. I think it's true to say that David Camp introduced her to Norman Atkins and was one of those who persuaded her to run as a federal candidate and certainly gave her every assistance he could and found people to help through the long arm of the Big Blue Machine."

Camp does not deny that Atkins' support was a great advantage for Campbell.

"He (Atkins) was Mulroney's campaign manager and had, and still has, probably, one of the larger networks in terms of party organization and people with various skills and aptitudes, probably more so than anybody I know of, because he keeps at it, he keeps in touch."

However, Atkins plays down his role in Campbell's career. "I don't think that her relationship with me did anything to move her all that far, but maybe it did. I think what she's done, she's done on her own ability to impress people within the system."

Atkins is equally enthusiastic about Campbell. "I saw her as a woman from the West. I knew her, I liked her, I mean she was my candidate before she was her own candidate. I wasn't that close to her but I saw her as a person for whom the time had clearly come to seek the national leadership."

He says he began to consider Campbell as a successor to Mulroney "from the time that there was speculation that Brian Mulroney might be stepping down."

Atkins says he didn't work on Campbell's campaign, but neither did he make any secret of his views. However there are indications that his role was more active than he admits. Graham Fraser of the *Globe and Mail* suggested during the run-up to the leadership convention that Atkins was intimidating Campbell's potential opponents into withdrawing.

> *Apparently unasked, Senator Norman Atkins has been telling people considering running or their supporters that they will be 'humiliated.'*
> *Supporters of Mr. Charest were complaining that Mr. Atkins was arguing that the party would be served best by a rally around Ms Campbell.*
> *But the bitterest feelings are felt among supporters of Barbara McDougall.*
> *For a week ago — the evening of International Women's Day, one Tory noted sourly — Mr. Atkins came over to the table at Hy's in Ottawa, where two McDougall supporters, Denise Cole and Rita Mezzannotte, were dining.*
> *Ms Coles insists that Mr. Atkins' advice that Ms McDougall withdraw was given "out of concern for Barbara."*

> *"It was not done to intimidate," she said. "It was a conversation among friends." However, word of the encounter spread fast among admirers of Ms McDougall, who were furious with Mr. Atkins for making the argument, and argued that he was using his reputation as a former Tory campaign chairman to try to regain influence with the Campbell group.*

A few days after Campbell was appointed to the justice portfolio, Jeffrey Simpson of the *Globe and Mail* became the first journalist to predict she would succeed Mulroney.

"If you have a spare dime and are looking for a bet, place 10 cents on Kim Campbell to lead the Conservative Party some day," Simpson wrote on February 27, 1990.

"Named Justice Minister last week after only 15 months in federal politics, Ms Campbell has suddenly become the Tory to watch in Ottawa. Not since a fellow named Pierre Trudeau burst onto the federal scene in 1965 has a newcomer been catapulted so fast into the justice portfolio, traditionally a senior portfolio in the federal cabinet."

In the small world of Canadian political journalism, it doesn't take much to start a bandwagon rolling. Before long, Simpson's prediction was being echoed elsewhere, as in the feature story by Charlotte Gray which appeared in *Chatelaine* in September 1990:

> *These are heady times for Kim Campbell, the first female Minister of Justice. Ask*

> *anyone in Ottawa or her native Vancouver about the brisk 43-year-old who holds one of the biggest jobs in the federal cabinet, and you hear every cliché for a fast mover: "A woman to watch," "Canada's answer to Margaret Thatcher," "A minister on the fast track." The Globe and Mail's Jeffrey Simpson (a columnist renowned for lofty skepticism) announced he is prepared to bet 10 cents on Kim Campbell to lead the Conservative Party some day.*
>
> *It seems almost churlish, in this gush of high opinions and expectations, to question the received wisdom.*

Indeed, no one did question the received wisdom. What's striking about the media treatment of Campbell from 1990 to early 1993 is the near unanimity with which she was hailed as the living embodiment of every desirable political attribute. The problematic areas — inexperience, skimpy credentials — were simply ignored. A couple of columnists who did write critical pieces stuck out like bouncers at a Sunday School picnic. The standard tone became one of awe-struck admiration, as in this passage by Greg Weston.

> *At 42, she is a dedicated workaholic, highly educated, a deep intellectual, a tough negotiator, articulate, witty, congenial. She is bright. Extremely bright.*
>
> *She is fluent in French, English and Russian and is described by friends and*

> *associates as an extraordinary "quick study" who can absorb enormous amounts of complicated material. Some say she has a photographic memory. She is a member of the Mensa organization for geniuses.*

Campbell took the trouble to deny that she belonged to Mensa, apparently feeling this elitist connection was not advantageous, but she didn't bother to correct the many other inaccuracies which made her record seem better than it was.

David Taras, a political scientist at the University of Calgary, says the Canadian media didn't do their job in examining Campbell's credentials.

"Nobody asked the tough questions," says Taras. "She was let through the line without the kind of scrutiny that U.S. presidential candidates get, for example."

He says Canadians were shocked when they saw Campbell perform in the television debates during the leadership race, so great was the contrast between what they saw and what they had been led to expect. "She doesn't come across well on television at all; she looks worried and sounds shrill."

Robert Fife says that Campbell began preparing to succeed Mulroney in the summer of 1992, a full year before the prime minister resigned. The implication is that Campbell knew Mulroney's resignation was imminent — a crucial bit of information that the press and the other potential leadership contenders did not have.

CHAPTER 18

OUR LADY OF THE HELICOPTERS

Anyone pursuing Frank Davies' analogy between Kim Campbell and Anne of Green Gables might have some difficulty with Campbell's phase as defence minister. It's hard to imagine a grown-up Anne defending the acquisition of 50 sub-hunting helicopters as Campbell was obliged to do after being named to succeed Marcel Masse in the defence portfolio.

It could hardly have been a job that she welcomed. Polls suggested the deal was opposed by two-thirds of Canadians, including 80 per cent of those in Campbell's home province.

However, by placing Campbell in charge of a department associated with traditionally male activities such as shooting and bombing, Mulroney helped build up her image as a woman of extraordinary capabilities. Presumably, a woman who is tough enough to be defence minister must be a tough cookie indeed.

This was a time when people were talking about the peace dividend — the hypothetical windfall that would result from the end of the Cold War as resources were shifted from the arms race to productive purposes. Campbell made short work of that notion: "In viewing what's been going on in the Soviet Union and Eastern Europe I think it's highly premature to beat our swords into ploughshares," she said.

The military community, accustomed to neglect, hoped that Campbell would be able to give it a place in the limelight.

"The only way the Department of National Defence could have a higher profile these days is if one of their search and rescue aircraft spotted Elvis Presley in a life raft," chortled defence analyst Martin Shadwick.

One aspect of the appointment escaped attention: As defence minister, Campbell would be in a position to oversee the implementation of the new policies on gays and lesbians in the military — the very policies she had stick-handled past the family caucus as justice minister.

Defence has traditionally not been a prominent post within the federal cabinet, but Campbell's move was generally heralded as a promotion.

"Ms Campbell's appointment was by far the biggest news in what was otherwise a workmanlike New Year's cabinet shuffle," commented the *Globe and Mail*. "In becoming Canada's first woman defence minister the former Soviet studies scholar inherits a budget of $12 billion and a wealth of potential photo opportunities."

Lisa Fiterman of the *Vancouver Sun* announced that Campbell had become "a legitimate contender for leadership of the Progressive Conservative Party" and took note of reports that Campbell's supporters were already conducting "a quiet telephone campaign across the country."

Campbell's "new-found muscles from pumping iron are but a tangible example of the power she wields in government," said Fiterman.

Fife points out a little-noted advantage of getting a double ministry, defence and veterans' affairs: Campbell had a double political staff to work on her leadership campaign.

Still, there were those helicopters. Even for a government with vast experience in ramming through unpopular decisions, the EH-101 was a hard sell. At a time when many Canadians were scratching to pay the bills or lining up at food banks, the helicopters would cost $5.8 billion over 15 years with inflation factored in.

Most people accept that the Armed Forces should be well-equipped for peacekeeping, search-and-rescue and surveillance of coastal waters, but they also know from painful experience that defence procurement is a quagmire of political patronage and corruption.

The Conservatives' first term in office had been dominated by scandals associated with the $1.2 billion Oerlikon low-level air-defence system. Government officials said the system was needed to protect Canadian troops and airfields in Europe, but by the time the units were in production the strategic situation had totally changed, and Canada was shutting down its military bases in Europe. It had been predicted that the Oerlikon deal would produce thousands of jobs since Canada would have the world product mandate for the system, but not a single unit was exported.

The Anglo-Italian EH-101 helicopter deal involved much higher expenditures and was even more controversial. The helicopter had been designed to counter the threat of Soviet submarines, but the collapse of the Soviet Union made that threat somewhat hypothetical. In the 1990s, the major issue relating to Soviet submarines is how to decommission aging reactors so they won't wind up as radioactive time bombs.

Recognizing the implausibility of the submarine threat, the government emphasized the search and rescue role of the helicopters. However, only 15 of the 50 helicopters were intended for search and rescue, and the EH-101 aircraft had not been designed for that role in any case. There was concern that the powerful downdraft from their rotors would drown anyone they were trying to rescue at sea.

The deal aroused further suspicion due to some of the people promoting it. Fred Doucet, a Mulroney pal from university days, worked as a lobbyist for Paramax Systems, the U.S.-controlled company which serves as main contractor for the EH-101. Bill Neville, who supervised the prime minister's office in the first months of the Mulroney government, also lobbied for the contract. Marcel Masse was defence minister when the deal was negotiated and Paramax is based in his home town of Montreal. Paul Manson headed the armed forces while the helicopter deal was taking shape, then became president of Paramax. In the end, huge sums of taxpayers' money were committed without a public tendering process.

In June, 1992, the Department of National Defence signed a $50,000 contract with a company called Advance Planning and Communications run by Tory insider Paul Curley to provide "communications plans" on the helicopter announcement. A copy of the contract released under the Access to Information Act is stuffed with jargon about "analyzing the environment on the helicopter issue from a communications perspective" and "developing strategic communications outlines" but what it comes down to is that Curley's people were getting $50,000 to sell the deal to Canadians.

Sean Moore, editor of the *Lobby Monitor*, an Ottawa publication that follows the lobbying industry, calls the Department of National Defence contract with Curley "bizarre" and "highly unusual." The Department had its own public relations staff capable of doing exactly the sort of thing that Curley's firm was hired to do. The contract covered six weeks of work, so Curley's firm was making more than $8,000 a week advising the Defence Minister on how to sell the deal. Perhaps it was Curley who provided Campbell with such persuasive lines as: "To have frigates without shipboard helicopters is like having an aircraft carrier without aircraft . . . you can't build a car and say, 'Sorry, we can't put the wheels on it.'" The metaphor is a bit misleading: just because the frigates were designed to carry sub-hunting helicopters doesn't mean either the frigates or the helicopters are needed to hunt subs. The real question is whether Canadian security is threatened by enemy submarines.

Handling the helicopter issue, Campbell demonstrated her capacity to take a lot of flak, an attribute which no doubt endeared her to party strategists. Cynics might suggest that the prime function of an elected Tory is to take heat for the unpopular deals concocted in the party's back rooms. Campbell had demonstrated her thick skin as Vancouver School Board chairman, making herself the willing target for public outrage over unpopular policies which she had no part in developing. Now she found herself carrying the can for the helicopters, and did so willingly, knowing that the party's power brokers were backing her as the next prime minister. She had to pay her dues.

Campbell emerged from the debate unscathed, judging by the media coverage. The impression left in the public mind was that she defended the deal because she had been assigned to do so, while the people actually responsible for it had conveniently made themselves scarce. The helicopter purchase would have been much more explosive if it had been defended by Marcel Masse since there would inevitably have been charges that Masse was steering federal money to Montreal where Paramax is based.

Campbell's appointment as defence minister sparked what might be considered her most daring quote of all: "Who needs a leadership race? I'll just stage a military coup. Don't mess with me, I have tanks."

The federal government bans ordinary citizens from joking about hijackings in airports but apparently it's acceptable for the defence minister to joke about launching a military coup.

CHAPTER

19

CAMPBELLMANIA

To understand the psychology of a nation is to hold the keys to power, and it could be argued that Campbell rode to power by exploiting one of the most powerful complexes in the Canadian collective consciousness, a cluster of buzzing neurons labeled: nostalgia for the Trudeau era.

From the time that she first attracted national attention, her backers constantly compared her with Trudeau and the analogy was often picked up by political journalists, as in this piece by Julian Beltrame of *Southam News:*

> *Get ready for Campbell-mania.*
> *Not since Pierre Trudeau exploded on the national scene in 1968 has a rookie politician aroused so much excitement, publicity and yes, "hope for change" as the fast-talking blonde from Lotusland.*
> *The Tory leadership race hasn't officially begun, but already the 45-year-old chess-*

playing, cello-bowing lawyer is so hot her staff is turning away interviews, fearing overexposure, and this has nothing to do with her now famous bared-shouldered photograph.

And the person Avril Phaedra Campbell — she adopted Kim at age 12 — is most compared to is Pierre Elliott Trudeau.

Just look at the adjectives used to describe Trudeau — and now trotted out to fit Campbell:

Flippant. Super-bright. Arrogant. Elitist. Combative. Funny. Even sexy, although that last one has mostly come from the British tabloids, which have dubbed her Canada's Madonna.

Campbell's witty riposte: "To compare me to Madonna is like comparing a strapless evening gown to a gownless evening strap."

The comparisons with Trudeau don't end there. The former prime minister was fluently bilingual; Campbell is trilingual or quadrilingual, adding Russian and a smattering of German to her linguistic arsenal. Trudeau traveled to China; Campbell spent three months in Russia studying the Soviet Union's economy. Trudeau was called a philosopher king; Campbell quotes Plato and reads Tolstoy and Dostoevsky.

Both studied at the London School of Economics, both used ground-breaking and generally applauded policies at jus-

> *tice to propel themselves to the top, both at the tail end of their first term in federal politics.*

The Trudeau-Campbell analogy has been mentioned so frequently that it deserves closer examination. How much do Campbell and Trudeau really have in common?

When Trudeau arrived on the federal scene in 1965 he had a law degree like Campbell and like her had spent time at the London School of Economics. So far so good. However, he also had a Master's degree in political science from Harvard, while she had never finished her Master's.

Trudeau had also studied at the Sorbonne and spoke both English and French flawlessly, something which linguists say is extremely rare. Campbell was frequently described as fluently bilingual during the run-up to the leadership race, but when she began touring in Quebec francophones had difficulty understanding her.

It is interesting to compare what Newman had to say about Campbell's French in his two reports about her.

In the article intended for general consumption, which was published in *Vancouver Magazine*, he said:

"The significance of music to her political incarnation hit me as I watched her speaking French to a national defence delegation in Ottawa last January, and quickly realized that even though she sounded letter-perfect and relaxed, she was reading every word and comma from a prepared text. What was remarkable about the performance was not so much her command of French as her mastery of its cadence. It's her musical ear as much as her mental agility that allows her to grasp foreign languages so rapidly and accurately."

The average person reading this passage would conclude that Campbell had an awesome and musical mastery of French. But in the confidential version of the article, which was released only to a select list of clients through a firm called RHA Information Services, Newman had this to say.

"Although she is billed as being bilingual, Kim's French is of the high-school variety and what saves it is her musical ear. Her accent and cadence are near perfect; her vocabulary is barely adequate."

As events have proved, the second version is the accurate one. However, even the second version gives her higher marks in French than would a high school oral exam. While Campbell's cadence and accent may be impressive for an anglophone, they are by no means "near perfect." The question arises: If Newman believed his confidential assessment of Campbell's French, why the sugar-coated public version?

When Trudeau came to Ottawa he had already built a reputation as one of the leading thinkers of his generation in Quebec. For 10 years he edited his own newspaper, *Cité Libre*, which was a significant force in the intellectual and cultural ferment known as the Quiet Revolution.

Campbell hasn't published anything except for her high school poetry and a facetious essay in the

UBC student newspaper. As UBC professor Philip Reznick puts it, "You will not find the collected works of Kim Campbell. They don't exist."

Much of Trudeau's mystique arose from his reputation as an athlete and adventurer. He was a master of wilderness canoeing and had traveled around the world alone, carrying nothing but a knapsack. Apart from her trips at the expense of the Canada Council, Campbell had seen little of the world prior to entering politics.

Trudeau began his political career as a left-wing activist fighting the authoritarian regime of Quebec premier Maurice Duplessis. He was at the side of the miners in the bitter Asbestos strike, urging them to resist oppression, negotiating for them, and providing free legal advice.

Campbell began her political career as president of the UBC frosh society, whose sole purpose was to organize social events. She went on to the Vancouver School Board, where she was preoccupied with cutting school budgets, and finally drove the teachers to an illegal strike. Campbell has always sought to ally herself with those in power.

When Trudeau arrived in Ottawa, he had basically never failed at anything he had tried. This contributed to his aura of confidence and arrogance.

Campbell was a failed academic who could not get a regular job at a small community college.

Trudeau first attracted national attention when he introduced legislation liberalizing the laws on divorce, abortion and homosexuality in December 1967. He established his presence with a single quip: "The state has no place in the bedrooms of the nation."

Campbell failed to win caucus approval for legislation to include sexual orientation as a prohibited grounds for discrimination in the Canadian Human Rights Act. Her abortion bill died in the Senate. Her gun control bill did not ban the type of gun that was used in the Polytechnique massacre. Her rape-shield legislation is innovative, but remains to be tested in the courts, and a number of prominent criminal lawyers have condemned it as unworkable.

Use of the term Campbellmania in news copy implied that Campbell produced a wave of excitement similar to Trudeaumania in 1968. However, the passion for Trudeau developed after the public had watched him perform at a televised leadership convention. In Campbell's case the so-called mania came before the convention, when few people had had a chance to watch her in action. For that matter, Campbellmania had no visible public manifestation — there were no cheering crowds, no rapturous outpourings of emotion such as those that characterized Trudeaumania at its height.

Finally, Trudeau had a clear vision of Canada as a just society with a strong federal government. The vision was never realized, and some thought it was crazy, but everybody knew what it was. Campbell, on the other hand, has never enunciated a vision of Canada. No one knows how she imagines the future. Her strongest theme is that the government must eliminate its deficit but she won't say how.

CHAPTER 20

LEADERSHIP RACE

The oddest thing about Campbellmania is that it had no visible cause. Campbell didn't do anything in the last week of February or the first week of March 1993 to spark the sudden outburst of media coverage which identified her in the public mind as a clear front-runner in the Conservative leadership race.

She had not delivered any dazzling speeches, nor made any policy announcements. The only thing that had happened was that Mulroney had resigned. She was the same person after the resignation as she had been before, yet with the existence of a job opening she suddenly became the media darling. For about three weeks following Mulroney's resignation the political press rallied around her as if by common accord, praising her to the sky and largely ignoring all the other potential contenders. Three weeks may not seem a long time, but this was the crucial period when leadership hopefuls were scrambling to assess their chances. Some of them must have been surprised to discover they had none, because Campbell was so far ahead. Geoffrey Stevens summarized the situation in the *Globe and Mail:*

> *If the news media were choosing the next leader of the Progressive Conservative Party, Kim Campbell would win on the first ballot.*
> *This is not because the sages of the fourth estate have made a shrewd and positive assessment of her political views (which are unknown, as yet, on most subjects), her experience (slight) or her performance (as justice minister, mixed; as defence minister, too soon to tell).*
> *Campbell is the early media favorite because in a less-than dazzling field, she seems at first glance to be the best exemplification of the "Clinton factor" — of the public's desire for change.*
> *In Campbell's case the proffered change is less a matter of generation (several other hopefuls are about her age, 45) than it is of gender. Electing a woman would be the boldest thing the federal Tories have ever done, ranking right up there with the dramatic gamble the Liberals took in 1968 when they chose Pierre Elliott Trudeau, then in his sandals-and-sports-car phase.*

Why was it that not a single journalist wrote a story hyping the virtues of Joe Clark as the leadership race got rolling? Clark has won the respect of Canadians the hard way, by playing fair, being gracious in defeat, serving in many thankless jobs and always seeking compromise. He is fluently bilingual, trusted by everyone, has never been involved in a scandal. Clark probably would have entered the race if he'd had anything like the kind of cheering section that Campbell had.

But there were no puff pieces for Clark, nor for Michael Wilson, Benoit Bouchard, Perrin Beatty, Barbara McDougall or Jean Charest. It was as if the press gallery had reached a consensus that Campbell was the right candidate to succeed Mulroney. How this happened is a genuine mystery. The odd thing is that the consensus of the press gallery coincided precisely with the opinion of the Tory insiders.

Julian Beltrame wrote on March 8, "Campbell's ability to attract such party brass as Senator Norman Atkins, who ran Mulroney's 1988 campaign, former party national director Paul Curley and lobbyist Bill Neville has established her as the clear choice of the Mulroney establishment."

Peter Newman reported to clients at RHA Information Services that the race was over before it had begun.

"There's never been a political phenomenon like it," said Newman.

"In the three weeks between Brian Mulroney's resignation and Kim Campbell's leadership declaration, Canada's political landscape was drastically altered. The British Columbia MP who joined the Progressive Conservative Party only four years ago, had become a shoe-in to win the party's mid-June leadership convention, thus making her the country's 19th — and first woman — prime minister."

When word got out that Mulroney's old friend Senator Guy Charbonneau was helping Campbell raise funds, the sense that the fix was in became overwhelming.

"The perception is that Mulroney is backing Campbell," said a Tory insider quoted in the *Ottawa Sun*, identified only as a close friend of the prime minister. "Kim Campbell now has Quebec locked up. It's all over."

A number of intelligent potential leadership candidates considered the situation and came to an intelligent conclusion — no one had a chance against Campbell. Michael Wilson bowed out despite $3 million in pledges from Bay Street. Barbara McDougall stepped aside with partially contained fury. Don Mazankowski and Benoit Bouchard took a tandem leap into retirement.

Although there were bitter complaints in private, the only Tory who vented his frustration publicly was Patrick Boyer. "If this thing wasn't so serious it would almost be high farce," he said, adding that the "laying on of hands for Campbell" was "totally outside of any democratic procedure."

When Perrin Beatty announced on March 16 that he would not run for the leadership, the situation had become highly embarrassing for the Mulroneyites. Mulroney had wanted a graceful, non-divisive transfer of power to his preferred candidate, but he did not want a coronation.

Canada is a democracy not a banana republic where the outgoing leader designates his successor. The optics were all wrong. There had never been such a thing in Canadian history. Patrick Doyle of the *Toronto Star* reported gleefully that the Tories were considering calling off their convention. The mood within the party can be glimpsed in a column by Michel Gratton of the *Ottawa Sun:*

> *One after another the Tory heavy hitters dropped by the wayside.*
> *Not only don't they want any part of the game, they're disgusted with the way it appears to have been rigged for Kim Campbell in the first place. In a weird way, this is looking more like a party revolt than a leadership race. One would think Campbell would be delighted that it all came to her so easily. In fact, insiders say she feels terrible about what is happening too far, too fast.*

Gratton's reference to a "party revolt" is insightful. In non-democratic countries, opposition parties often refuse to run in elections because to do so would lend legitimacy to a process they consider fraudulent. No loyal Tory would publicly denounce the prime minister, but the decision by major players with known leadership ambitions to stay out of the race may have been one way for them to show what they thought of the way it was being run.

The dilemma for the Mulroney machine was acute. To forgo a leadership convention would be unthinkable. Conventions provide reams of publicity, create the impression of change and renewal and are almost always followed by a surge in popularity for the winning candidate. What would it say about the Conservative Party if only one serious candidate could be found? An opponent for Campbell had to be found.

It would have been fascinating to listen in on the conversations that took place between Mulroney and Jean Charest at this time. Charest had not been taken seriously in his role as environment minister, as was shown by his exclusion from the most powerful cabinet committees, but now Mulroney needed him desperately. There have been reports that Mulroney promised to help Charest in financing his campaign and it would be interesting to know the details of the arrangement.

Charest obviously did not want to be a sacrificial lamb, sent into the ring merely to generate a bit of excitement. If he entered the race, he wanted to believe he had an honest chance of winning. Mulroney must have convinced him he had that chance.

CHAPTER

21

VICTORY

Ottawa motorists plying their daily errands on the weekend of the Tory leadership convention in mid-June might have been startled by a strange apparition among the muffler shops and pizza joints on Bank Street. It was Kim Campbell's hospitality tent, but it looked like something out of Camelot, perhaps the battlefield headquarters of King Arthur himself. A fanciful edifice of fluorescent pink and white, planted directly across from the hockey arena where the convention would take place, the Campbell tent dominated the scene in the same way that her organization dominated the convention floor. Its dazzling colors were echoed in the myriad of Kim buttons, Kim umbrellas, Kim shirts and Kim hats worn by the delegates milling about in the hot sunshine. Here at last was the visible manifestation of Campbellmania and proof of what money can buy.

One would never have guessed that this candidate was dedicated to eliminating waste and restoring frugality. "Beside her (Campbell) Charest is like a *Pelagie-la charette* who sells his hot dogs on the street," wrote Nathalie Petrowski of *La Presse*. "His tent is so far from the action you practically need an airplane to get there and his supporters are so agitated that the violent green of their official t-shirt winds up getting confused with the lawn."

The bright colors and festive atmosphere did not reflect the reality of Campbell's campaign which had been dogged by trouble almost from the moment that she officially entered the race.

It seemed that Campbell and her advisers had became the victims of their own success by creating expectations which no human being could fulfill.

Charest, the last-minute candidate, turned out to be a far more engaging personality than the public expected. He was extremely articulate in both languages and had a good sense of humor. He remembered people's names, he had an intact family (which may not be a liability even in the 1990s), and had a lot of energy.

It would be going too far to portray Charest as the ideal prime minister who got away. His record as environment minister was basically one of all talk and no action, although this may reflect his lack of influence in cabinet rather than lack of sincerity. No one can deny that he is a likable person. He seems to genuinely like his fellow man and woman rather than considering them as rabble who are incapable of rational thought.

Neither Campbell nor Charest offered substantive policies and it was clear that Mulroney had set some firm ground rules about respecting the party's established policies. The choice therefore became one based on personalities, and on these grounds there really was no contest. Charest was a warm human being who had a simple, uncomplicated past. His father was a pro-hockey player, his wife was beautiful, his children were cute, everywhere he went people took to him.

By the time of the convention, the public mood had swung overwhelmingly to Charest. A Gallup Poll on the eve of the convention suggested that, if an election had been held at that time, the Tories would have won with him as leader but not with Campbell. Charest's supporters were clearly in high spirits as they poured into the Ottawa Civic Centre on June 13. Charest looked confident as he waited for voting results surrounded by his parents, wife, children, brother and various in-laws. His little daughter danced excitedly on the bench.

However, anyone looking down on the convention floor could not help but notice the predominance of Campbell supporters. Two thirds of the people seemed to be wearing Kim's colors and waving her placards.

When the first ballot results were announced, the change in mood was dramatic. All the color drained from Charest's face as he stared into space, stunned. He knew it was all over even though the voting would go to a second ballot. It took another hour or so before his daughter realized that he had lost and burst into tears.

Media commentary on Campbell's victory was sometimes savage, as in this post-mortem by Allan Fotheringham:

> *After being out-campaigned by Jean Charest throughout the leadership race, she won in Ottawa only because the money and organization supplied by the party brass sewed up delegates early and kept them under tight control once at the convention.*
> *The Campbell organizers have been boasting (unwisely) to reporters since the convention how they manipulated the event and out-gunned the underfunded Charest workers.*
> *Those such as Paul Curley, a remnant of Ontario's Big Blue Machine, has explained how his Campbell troops practically "captured" convinced and uncommitted delegates as soon as they arrived in the city, held them as long as possible with minders and handlers in Campbell's headquarters hotel, the Westin, and stroked them with booze and food.*
> *The idea, of course, was to create the impression that the Campbell candidacy was unstoppable, and far ahead — when in fact it was leaking badly.*
> *There were 3,846 delegates eligible to vote but there were another 1,965 alternates.*
> *In the steamy ice rink there were in addition probably 2,000-3,000 Tory volun-*

> *teers, groupies and youthful rent-a-mob cheerleaders assembled by the Campbell money and clout.*
> *To create the impression of a coming Campbell landslide, there was a waving sea of hot pink Campbell banners and signs as delegates entered the arena — an impression that disguised the fact that only a portion of those waving the banners could vote.*
> *Only a third of those in the hockey rink could vote — the rest were props to fool the TV cameras and the "uncommitted."*

Patrick Boyer came to Charest's camp even though he knew Charest would not win, giving a strong signal of Boyer's feelings about Campbell. When Campbell's victory was officially announced, Joe Clark did not clap, and some reporters noted that even Mulroney had a furrow in his brow.

It was widely rumored that by the end of the leadership race he had lost his enthusiasm for Campbell. He did not go to the stage to congratulate her as outgoing leaders usually do.

Many Charest supporters were bitter at the outcome. "I walked out of this convention feeling that the party had made a mistake," says Lindsay Blackett, a young Conservative who has worked on several campaigns. "Charest was the better candidate but the party elite decided that this was the way it was going to be."

Blackett says that the party elite pressured a lot of people to vote for Kim Campbell before people had a chance to know her. "You look at people like Bill Neville and Dalton Camp; it doesn't take a rocket scientist to figure it out. They made a lot of money during the Mulroney era and they want the gravy train to continue. I don't believe they looked that deeply into Campbell's record because if they had they would have seen what everybody else has seen."

Blackett says the Campbell organization paid an accreditation fee of $575 for each of 600 non-voting observers (for a total of $345,000) whose sole purpose was to wave banners and create the impression of enthusiastic support for Campbell on the campaign floor. Surprising though it may seem, Blackett says many delegates are influenced by such tactics, because they want to be on the winning side. It is likely that these "observers" actually cost more than the price of admission. They may have been "entertained" at some expense to make it more worth their while. The Charest campaign also paid the fees for some observers, but it could only afford twenty, Blackett says.

Charest supporters allege that Campbell spent about $3 million on her campaign, most of it on air fare and accommodation for delegates. That would be roughly triple the official spending limit of $900,000. Campaign spending figures have not yet been released.

Campbell supporters don't deny that superior organization was crucial in her victory.

"Leadership campaigns by definition are exercises in winning delegates one at a time," says

Bill Neville, one of the powerful and well-connected lobbyists who worked for Campbell's campaign.

"Speeches and all those things are wonderful but what you really need is people on the ground and there's no question, particularly as it played out, that her superior strength in organizational terms was an important factor in her winning."

It's interesting to note that Neville and Paul Curley, another prominent lobbyist, donated their services to Campbell's campaign free of charge. According to Sean Moore of the *Lobby Monitor*, top lobbyists charge $2,000 to $3,000 a week for their services. If a top lobbyist donates a month of time, that's $8,000 to $12,000 which doesn't have to be declared by the candidate when filing campaign expenses. If there are several lobbyists involved, as there were in Campbell's campaign, the impact can be significant. Moore believes these voluntary contributions should have to be declared under the regulations governing lobbying activities.

Neville says there's no need for him to make a formal declaration because his involvement in Campbell's campaign was public knowledge anyway. Actually, there was some confusion surrounding Neville's involvement in Campbell's campaign. His name does not appear on a list of campaign organizers made public by Campbell's office. How long was he in fact involved, and how deeply? There were rumors that he was running the show. Both Neville and Curley were also active in lobbying for the EH-101 helicopter deal.

CHAPTER

22

CREDENTIALS

The Canadian voter is in a predicament something like that of the ancient Greek philosopher who went to the market in broad daylight with his lantern burning, searching for an honest person.

Simple honesty may not be the only quality needed in a prime minister but without it all the other virtues aren't much good. If intelligence is employed to pursue a hidden agenda, it is actually worse than stupidity.

The ethical tone of a government is set at the top. A prime minister cannot guarantee that all operations of government will be conducted with integrity, but he or she can stop large-scale abuses.

In this context Prime Minister Kim Campbell's habit of inflating her credentials is not reassuring. Prior to her election as chairman of the Vancouver School Board, the *Vancouver Sun* reported, based on information supplied by Campbell, that she had her Master's Degree from the London School of

Economics. When running in the 1983 provincial election, Campbell released a resume saying she traveled throughout Asia, Europe and South America, but there is no period in her life when such extensive travels could have taken place because by her own account she was doing other things. Although her trip to the Soviet Union would mean she had been to a part of Asia, the word "throughout" suggests a tour more extensive than a visit to single country.

In recent years both *Chatelaine* and *Saturday Night* reported that Campbell had her Master's degree. Quality magazines like these have fact-checkers who go over each article verifying significant facts with the author's sources. Charlotte Gray, the author of both articles, insists her information came directly from Campbell's office. Gray is a respected journalist who would not jeopardize her reputation by deliberately reporting false information.

A resume on file at the B.C. Legislature from the time Campbell was an MLA says she did graduate work at the University of Oregon in the summer of 1969, but *Maclean's* writers Janigan and Fulton established that this was not true. She had taken one undergraduate course.

Campbell has made no effort to correct erroneous media reports about her academic credentials although she has taken the trouble to correct errors of lesser significance from time to time. In 1991 she wrote the *Ottawa Citizen* to complain about an article suggesting she did not like the Canadian national anthem, and in 1993 she wrote the *Toronto Star* to deny a story suggesting she wanted to be a concert cellist.

One area of great confusion is language skills. There have been numerous published reports that Campbell speaks three languages: English; French; Russian and some stories add a fourth, German. In Peter Newman's famous *Vancouver Magazine* story, the list was further expanded:

> *Her most startling revelation during our lunch was that she speaks Yiddish, not what you might expect from the daughter of the hard-bitten Presbyterian-Scots couple who shared that sweet moment on the Port Alberni lookout. I knew that Campbell had mastered French, German and Russian, but it seems that last time she was in Toronto, she spent an evening with the Martin Goldfarbs (he polls for the Liberals) with Rosie Abella and her husband Irving, twin pillars of the local Jewish community. They were all talking about Yiddish because it is one of the hardest languages to learn because it is so derivative and colloquial. "I had the best vocabulary of any of them," Campbell remembers — and those who were there confirm it. (She picked it up from her first husband.)*

Anyone who has struggled for years to learn a second language cannot fail to be impressed by those rare people who speak three or four. Campbell's claimed multilinguism no doubt enhanced her image as super-intelligent. One of the most awkward moments in her campaign for the Tory leadership came when it was revealed, on CBC television, that she could not say "hello" in Russian. The painful episode came in an interview with Joe Schlesinger, who asked Campbell how she would greet Boris Yeltsin when he came to Vancouver. It was clear to anyone watching the interview that Campbell was taken unawares and could not respond.

Campbell's friend J.J. Camp later suggested she had never claimed to be multilingual. "She will tell you she is not a polyglot," said Camp in an interview with Rob Russo of *The Canadian Press*. "Her Russian is almost non-existent and her German is probably worse."

Questioned on the matter, Ray Castelli, manager of her leadership campaign, said Campbell's Russian skills needed refreshing. Castelli said in an interview he once suggested to Campbell she go to dinner with Mikhail Gorbachev who was visiting Canada.

"She was quite offended and said, 'I'm not the kind of prop that you wind up and say, Now here, speak Russian. My Russian is not that good. I can do that but I'm going to have to take an intensive three or four day refresher course full time to learn the language again and practice it.' I've never heard her brag about speaking Russian, and it's always made her uncomfortable when she sees it in print that she speaks fluent Russian.

"She does not claim nor have I ever heard her claim that she speaks fluent Russian right now. What she's always said to me, extremely consistently, is that she traveled across the Soviet Union by herself and had learned the language and could speak it and spoke it very well, and was able to travel the country without any help or assistance."

However, a curriculum vitae provided by Campbell's office during the 1993 election campaign states without qualification: "Languages Spoken: English, French and Russian." The resume does not say she once spoke Russian. It uses the present tense to suggest the skill is active and current. As for the claim that she traveled through the Soviet Union alone, anyone who visited that country when it was still intact knows that Westerners were not allowed to travel freely and unaccompanied. They were shepherded through in groups following carefully set itineraries, accompanied by guides who acted as translators.

Phil Rankin recalls discussing Campbell's language skills in their school board days.

"She always maintained to me that she spoke Russian so fluently that when she traveled for her 60 days' journey in the Soviet Union she could virtually submerge herself in the population, her Russian was so good. Well I spoke to her Russian professor about it, because I knew it was just ludicrous, and she laughed. It's ridiculous. She's taken something like a second-year Russian course at UBC. She can read the alphabet. She can't speak Russian at all. I think if anyone spoke to her even in the most basic Russian she could probably say, '*Da, spaceba,*' or something. I can say that too. She can say perestroika with a better accent than I can.

"She maintained to me she spoke Yiddish because her husband spoke Yiddish. I spoke Yiddish too when I was young but I know she doesn't speak Yiddish. When we were on the school board Polly Weinstein (former Vancouver School Board chairman) was forever saying little Yiddish things and she (Campbell) wasn't getting it."

Janigan and Fulton say in *Maclean's*, "She presents herself as a determined woman who has excelled at almost everything she has attempted. But . . . she has enhanced that sunny image by adroitly concealing details and editing facts. And when she recounts her achievements she often takes subtle credit for more than she has actually accomplished. Although she has often disputed unflattering accounts of her experiences, she has not corrected frequently erroneous reports that she has postgraduate degrees in political science. She has also been credited with proficiency in German, Russian, French and, most recently, Yiddish — but only her French is at the functional level."

When I asked Campbell's staff about the false information in the resumes, the answer came back: "They were not written by her. Why would she claim false academic credentials in political races when being discovered has such a high price?"

It's a good question.

CHAPTER

23

PRIME MINISTER KIM

Joy was written all over Kim Campbell's face as she posed for photographers after the swearing in of her new cabinet. But the *Reuters* photographer captured something else. Her hand was planted firmly on the thigh of her defence minister, Tom Siddon.

In the 1988 election, then Liberal leader John Turner was ridiculed from coast to coast for bum-patting. To be sure, a pat on the knee is not the same thing as a pat on the bum. Sexual harassment is very much in the eyes of the "touchee." Harassment is considered especially offensive if the aggressor holds a position of authority over the person harassed, and a prime minister clearly holds power over her ministers, yet Campbell's gesture passed without criticism. To be fair, Siddon did not object to having his leg patted, judging from the broad smile on his face. However, women have been campaigning against touching in the workplace and for a prime minister to touch a subordinate sets a dubious example. To add to the psychological complexities, he had been her boss when she first arrived in Ottawa.

A number of feminists questioned about the gesture said they would object if a man placed his hand on their knee in a similar situation, yet saw nothing objectionable about Campbell placing her hand on Siddon's knee. It appears there is a double standard when it comes to harassment, but it may be a legitimate double standard. The reality is that men and women have different responses to being touched. The odd thing is that this highly debatable issue passed without any debate.

The new cabinet was cobbled together from Mulroney-era remnants and Campbell's leadership rivals. The most striking thing about it was the lack of experienced personnel. Many of the new ministers were unknown outside their home regions. Jeffrey Simpson of the *Globe and Mail* called it "the weakest Canadian cabinet in a generation."

Ontarians were galled at what they considered drastic under-representation of their province. The *Toronto Star* complained to Campbell that, "The country's biggest city has been relegated to a political backwater in your cabinet. Only one, low-profile politician from the area, Scarborough's Pauline Browes, made it as minister of Indian affairs — a portfolio that hardly resonates with Toronto's challenges." Ontario Premier Bob Rae retaliated by boycotting Campbell's first meeting with the premiers held in Vancouver claiming that it was too far to go for a photo-op. The Atlantic premiers came only after Campbell sent a federal jet to pick them up.

Quebec Premier Robert Bourassa made the day by showing up — it would appear that the special Tory relationship with Quebec would continue under Campbell despite her inadequate French. The Quebec business community was pleased with the helicopter contract since the aerospace industry is based in Montreal. The crucial finance portfolio was given to Gilles Loiselle, a former Pequiste who was once René Lévesque's agent-general in London. As the *Ottawa Citizen* noted, "He has always taken the position that the smaller and less powerful the federal government becomes, the more he likes it. As finance minister, Loiselle is uniquely placed to promote that view. He will cut the federal deficit by cutting federal spending with special enthusiasm all his own." As for Garth Turner, would-be leader of the tax revolt, he was put in charge of collecting taxes.

It would take more than a new-look cabinet to make people forget Mulroney-era sleaze, especially since four Tory MPs had been charged with fraud and influence peddling.

One of them, Maurice Tremblay, had been convicted and announced he would not seek re-election, but the other three — Carole Jacques, Gilles Bernier and Gabriel Fontaine — were still awaiting trial. Campbell announced she would not let them run as Tory candidates, but others criticized the decision, noting that Canadian law presumes a person is innocent until proven guilty.

Campbell's approach to federal-provincial relations seems identical to Mulroney's with the emphasis on decentralization rather than on a strong central government and on striking bargains rather than setting principles. A good example is her agreement with Quebec Premier Robert Bourassa to give Quebec control over job training in return for Quebec withholding criticism of the Canadian Environmental Assessment Act.

This secret deal fell through, apparently because Campbell got cold feet after Reform Party leader Preston Manning accused her of implementing the Charlottetown Accord on a piecemeal basis. The upshot is that no one knows what Quebec and Ottawa have agreed to concerning job training, and the vitally important business of environmental assessment of major projects remains swamped in confusion.

This point may need emphasis. The Canadian Environmental Assessment Act has been in the works for more than seven years. It has been subject to consultations in both the Commons and the Senate. For the past year a multi-stakeholder group including representatives of industry, the provincial governments and the environmental community, has been struggling to reach a consensus on what the rules should be for assessing new projects with a potential impact on the environment. After much negotiation and compromise on all sides, and after tens of millions of dollars in expense to the public purse, a consensus on the regulations has been achieved. Both the Commons and the Senate have passed the act. All that is needed is a cabinet order for it to become law. But there is no cabinet order. Why not?

In some other areas, Campbell showed breathtaking decisiveness. She had barely entered office before she announced a sweeping reorganization of the federal government. Whole departments disappeared, others had major branches lopped off and a few grew to gargantuan proportions. Fifty-three top bureaucrats earning $98,000 to $128,900 a year were given the boot, but it was a soft boot since they would continue to receive full salary.

The new Department of Public Security sounded like a truly Orwellian creation, lumping together the RCMP with the Canadian Security and Intelligence Service, the Correctional Service, Customs and Immigration. The *Citizen* said that "including Immigration in the law-and-order department smells of demagoguery and prejudice."

One result of the reorganization was massive confusion within the bureaucracy. Whereas previously it had taken one or two phone calls to get a response to a question, now it took three or four. People with urgent petitions were not where their pleas should be addressed.

Since Canadians love to blame their problems on a bloated federal government the reorganization was greeted favorably in many quarters but within the civil service there was demoralization and panic. Many services important to the functioning of a modern state can only be delivered by bureaucrats. Campbell did not offer any analysis of how her reorganization would improve efficiency or how much money it would save.

Environmentalists were especially unhappy with the dismembering of the Environment Department. The Canadian Parks Service, which had accounted for 40 per cent of its activity, was lumped together with tourism in the Department of Canadian Heritage. "We're really concerned that they are going to destroy the Environment Department," said Elizabeth May of the Sierra Club. "The staff are just freaked out. Half of the assistant deputy ministers are being chopped. I think this is just the beginning. We're going to get to the point where it's irreversible."

One result of the scrambling of departmental responsibilities is that year-to-year comparisons of departmental budgets will become meaningless. Anyone hoping to confuse the press and the public about the nature of future budget cuts could scarcely improve on this strategy. Campbell described it as "the most significant downsizing and restructuring of government ever undertaken in Canada" and she wasn't exaggerating.

The *Vancouver Sun* warned that such sweeping changes should not be carried out on the eve of an election: "Even if Ms Campbell had a cost-benefit analysis to justify her plan, she does not yet have a mandate to make changes on such a massive scale — changes that are bound to affect morale in the civil service just when the need for stability is paramount."

But reducing the number of departments allowed Campbell to announce that she had reduced the size of the federal cabinet, a valuable symbolic achievement. That another 2,000 civil servants would lose their jobs was scarcely cause for worry except to the families directly affected. No one seemed to care about the consequences in reduced government services, lower quality government research and statistics, reduced ability to protect the environment and so on. Her task was to create the impression of a new era and in this she partly succeeded. She reinforced that impression with proposals to whittle down MPs' pensions, although these cannot be passed until the Commons is recalled.

Through the summer Campbell continued to travel the country as if in an election campaign, yet without proclaiming an election. The result was that she could charge most of her expenses to the taxpayers, whereas her opponents could not. No wonder the newspapers and airwaves brimmed over with images of Campbell doing happy things. No wonder her stock began to rise in the public opinion polls. Like it or not, public opinion is largely a function of media publicity.

Campbell showed that she could relate to the people like an old-style politician, flipping pancakes, appearing on open-line programs, jogging, pitching a baseball, kissing babies and doing the twist. She even disclosed a previously hidden capacity for self-deprecating humor: "The other day in Toronto I went to put on a suit that I had worn in Tokyo and could not wedge the prime ministerial bottom into the prime-ministerial skirt." In Quebec she tried on a vegetarian hat comprised of fresh fruits and vegetables and joked about her lack of time for hanky-panky.

The intention was obviously to break down the conception of Campbell as a cold-hearted elitist, and make people forget how much they liked Jean Charest. By coincidence or design, Charest virtually disappeared from public view following the leadership convention.

Of course, all her travels were at public expense and she didn't travel economy class. For example, when she was in Vancouver she stayed at the royal suite in the Pan Pacific Hotel, which rents for more than $2,000 a night. But on phone-in programs she talked about frugality, her accurate knowledge of the latest price for a litre of milk and left the impression that she still did her own shopping in order to be sure what things cost.

There is something ironic about a political candidate living in the height of luxury traveling the country at huge expense while preaching the gospel of tightened belts. In the meantime, Jean Chrétien traveled southern Ontario in a rented car, which was all the Liberals could afford. The media often ignored Chrétien while following Campbell like glue. Obviously the Prime Minister is more newsworthy than the leader of the opposition. But if the prime minister is dispensing photo opportunities rather than policy statements should the same rule apply? A long pre-election campaign guaranteeing a head start to one party would not appear overly democratic — especially when the opposition parties will have less to spend anyway and less air-time available on TV.

The remarkable thing about the photo-op strategy was that it worked. The steady bombardment of Kim Campbell images in friendly contexts produced similar results to blitz advertising for products emphasizing recognition over judgement. By the end of the pre-election period she had become the most popular leader in the history of Canadian polling — or close to it.

Is Campbell qualified to lead Canada? Critics would say she doesn't have a vision of Canada and she's not an independent thinker, but in another sense she is perfectly qualified. She is used to being directed by others and lacks a clear ideology that would constrain her actions. The evidence shows that she will do what she is assigned to do. If she is assigned to chop school board budgets she will do so. She can speak in favor of free access to abortion but if she is assigned to promote a bill that would restrict access to abortion she will do so. She may not have the slightest interest in helicopters but she will defend the decision to buy a few billion worth if that is what she is asked to do.

Campbell is ideally suited to serve the purposes of a political machine. The Big Blue Machine didn't go wrong with her.

CHAPTER

24

CONTRADICTIONS

From her first day at the helm of power, Campbell's administration was characterized by intractable contradictions. She won the leadership by promising the politics of inclusion. Yet her leadership victory was the result of old-style machine politics, in which the grass roots are turned into lawn clippings.

She was presented to Canadians as an agent of change, yet she had been involved in all the major policies which made the Mulroney government unpopular including free trade, the GST and the Charlottetown Accord.

She set herself up as an advocate of political reform, promising stricter rules on lobbying, and banned three Tory MPs who had been charged with fraud and influence-peddling from running again. Yet her own leadership campaign benefited from the voluntary services of prominent lobbyists who had earlier been hired by private-sector companies to promote the EH-101 helicopter deal.

She was supposedly in charge of burying the Mulroney era, yet she came to power in good part thanks to his help, and many of the people behind her had been with Mulroney.

Campbell's most famous single quote, by far, is: "Charisma without substance is a dangerous thing." Yet her period as prime minister has been overwhelmingly devoted to building up her charisma, while statements of substance have been few and far between.

Those few statements of substance often appear to contradict each other. On one hand she talks about cutting the deficit in five years but on the other hand she promises to protect social programs. For a time, her position on health-care user fees seemed to change every week.

Similar confusion surrounds virtually every policy announcement that Campbell has made. She said one day that she would transfer responsibility for job training to Quebec, but the next day this was denied and in the end no one knew just what had been agreed to.

She claims that Department of National Defence headquarters in Ottawa never received a copy of a press release announcing the death of a Somali citizen while in the custody of Canadian troops, but Department of National Defence officials flatly contradict her, saying the press release was indeed sent.

Laying claim to nationalist credentials, Campbell declared her indignation at U.S. cultural and economic domination, saying no other nation would put up with it. But she didn't announce any substantive measures to protect Canadian culture. CBC president Gérard Veilleux abruptly resigned apparently after learning that even more drastic cuts were in store for Canada's premier cultural institution. There were hints that the GST on books might be removed but these trial balloons went down like lead with Tory MPs.

"My constituents would be much more interested in not having their electricity bills or feminine hygiene products taxed," said Ontario MP Rene Soetens. "Books just don't rate."

There were reports that the Campbell administration had taken a heroic stand against split-edition American magazines which produce phony Canadian editions. In fact, *Sports Illustrated* was permitted to continue its split edition, and there was no ban on future split-edition magazines; rather they would have to get approval from Investment Canada, a Mulroney creation which has never turned down a foreign investment proposal.

Campbell said she was committed to protecting the social safety net, but she wouldn't promise to avoid further cuts in federal transfer payments which help the provinces pay for education, health care and welfare. That's like someone saying they are committed to drive a car, but not to filling the tank.

EPILOGUE

Following the brief downturn during the leadership campaign, Campbell returned to her place as media darling. Her endless photo-opportunities are followed as if real news were about to erupt at any time. Real news does not erupt but the warm and fuzzy images continue to proliferate.

As the clock ticked toward an election call the Conservatives could count on some significant advantages. Campbell's pre-campaign electioneering had positioned them well with little expense to the party. Because of their strong performance in the last election, they would get a larger share of free advertising than the other parties.

But the biggest advantage was delivered indirectly by a right-wing lobby group called the National Citizens' Coalition which successfully challenged a key election-spending rule in an Alberta lower court. The rule in question prevented third parties such as lobby groups from spending more than $1,000 to oppose or promote a party or candidate.

Although the electoral legislation is federal, the coalition challenged the restriction in an Alberta lower court. UBC law professor Philip Bryden says the coalition "went forum-shopping to find the most conservative jurisdiction in the land."

The Alberta judge agreed that the restriction on third-party advertising contravened the Charter of Rights. Chief Electoral Officer, Jean-

Pierre Kingsley, announced on August 19 that the ban would not be enforced pending an appeal.

This means that business groups who generally favor the Conservative agenda will be free to invest millions on campaign advertising as they did in the final days of the 1988 election campaign. Many political observers believe that the flood of pro-free-trade advertising by third parties turned the tide in the Tories' favor, and there is no reason why the same thing could not happen again.

Bryden says the federal government could have taken other steps to keep the legislation in force if it had really wanted to.

"The government could have referred the case to a federal court so they would have had a decision that would have run across all the provinces. They could have said, 'We'll seek a stay.' There were certainly other steps they could have taken."

The lack of controls on third-party spending make a mockery of Canada's election-financing rules by allowing a wealthy minority to buy disproportionate influence.

It's wrong to say that everyone detested Mulroney by the time he resigned. Close to twenty per cent still thought he was doing a great job, and it's not hard to guess which twenty per cent. The rich really did get richer during the Mulroney years and they did so thanks to policies which remain in place, and which Campbell shows every intention of pursuing.

If Canadians can once again be seduced by images without considering platforms and policies, then we have only ourselves to blame.

ABOUT THE AUTHOR

Dennis Bueckert is a Parliamentary reporter for *The Canadian Press*. He is a graduate of the Carleton School of Journalism. (Yes, he finished his thesis.) He is married with three children. He rides to work on a Raleigh Gator 12-speed (built in Montreal) summer and winter.